THE CONCISE

YACHTMASTER

GUIDE

The Concise Yachtmaster Guide

A study and revision aid, with exercises, for students of the RYA Coastal Skipper and Yachtmaster Offshore shore based courses

by Mike Bowyer

© Mike Bowyer 1988
British Library CIP Data
Bowyer, Mike
    Concise yachtmaster guide.
    1. Seamanship – For yachting
    I. Title
    623.88'223

    ISBN 0–7153–9056–2

Photoset and printed in Great Britain by
Redwood Burn Limited, Trowbridge, Wiltshire
for David & Charles plc
Brunel House, Newton Abbot, Devon

Published in the United States of America
by David & Charles Inc
North Pomfret Vermont 05053 USA

The Course

The aim of this book is to help those studying for the RYA Coastal Skipper and Yachtmaster Offshore examinations. This is the advanced examination and it is assumed that readers will have satisfactorily completed the Day Skipper and Watch Leader courses or have equivalent knowledge and experience, which would include sailing offshore in different conditions and at night.

Many parts of the earlier course, particularly those concerned with elementary seamanship, are not touched on in this syllabus. In other subjects the same ground is covered, but in greater depth and in these cases this book recaps earlier knowledge wherever this has been thought helpful to readers.

At the end of the shore based course there are three examination papers – one each in meteorology, rule of the road and navigation. There is also a test in signals covering morse and the international code. The RYA also set papers throughout the course based on continual assessment of the student's progress.

The final Coastal Skipper/Yachtmaster Certificate will only be awarded to the candidate who has successfully completed the shore based course, the practical course and a final oral examination, but a course completion certificate will be awarded at the end of the shore based course to those candidates who have successfully completed it.

The sea time necessary to take the practical course for Coastal Skipper/Yachtmaster consists of 50 days at sea (not continuous), 2,500 miles of sailing, 5 passages over 60 miles long, 2 passages as skipper and 2 night passages.

Questions and Exercises

At the end of each chapter are questions or navigation exercises with answers at the end of the book. All the navigation exercises are on Admiralty Practice Chart No. 5052 (Dover Strait) and readers should purchase a copy of the chart to complete the exercises.

Acknowledgements

Tidal information is reproduced from Reed's Nautical Almanac by kind permission of the publishers. The tidal curve on page 50 is Crown Copyright and reproduced from Reed's, based on Admiralty Publications with the permission of the Controller of Her Majesty's Stationery Office. The Customs form on p. 157 is also with the permission of H.M.S.O.

The Author

Mike Bowyer first went to sea as an apprentice in the Merchant Navy in 1947. He gained his Master's Foreign Going Certificate and was a navigating officer with the Union Castle Mail S.S. Co., Ltd. until 1962, when he left the sea to pursue a new career in teaching.

Now deputy head of a special school in the South of England, one of his many duties is introducing young people to the experience of sailing. As an Instructor for the RYA/DTI shore based Yachtmaster courses (both Offshore and Ocean) for over 20 years he has also introduced many adults to the sea.

Mike keeps an Achilles 24 in Cornwall, which he sails with his wife and young son. He has also cruised extensively in the Solent, English Channel, Scottish Waters and the Mediterranean. He is Chairman of the Berkshire branch of the Sail Training Association.

Contents

1

DEAD RECKONING AND ESTIMATED POSITION

It is essential that a skipper knows the position of the vessel at sea at all times and plots it on the chart. Methods by which positions may be found by taking bearings of navigational objects, or by radio bearings or electronic instruments are dealt with in later chapters, but the first section of the syllabus is concerned with plotting the progress of a passage without those fixes by the two methods of dead reckoning and estimated position.

First revise this elementary chartwork.

Describing position

A ship's position can be given in latitude and longitude or as a bearing and distance off a named point. In the former case always use latitude first, then longitude, using both degrees and minutes. **Example**: Latitude 50 25'N Longitude 5 40'W, always shortened to 50 25'N 5 40'W. Latitude scale is at the two sides of the chart, longitude scale along top and bottom.

The latitude of a place on the surface of the earth is the angular distance of that place north or south of the equator. The angle is measured from the centre of the earth to the plane of the meridian through that place. It is given in degrees, from 0 to 90, subdivided by 60 minutes to each degree and 60 seconds to each minute.

A parallel of latitude is a small (so called) circle whose plane is parallel to the plane of the Equator. On the diagram places that have the same latitude as A lie on that parallel of latitude or small circle. In the top diagram, C represents the centre of the earth, A is a place on the earth's surface, PABP a meridian passing through A, and ACB the angle of latitude at the centre of the earth.

Longitude is the angular distance between a place on the surface

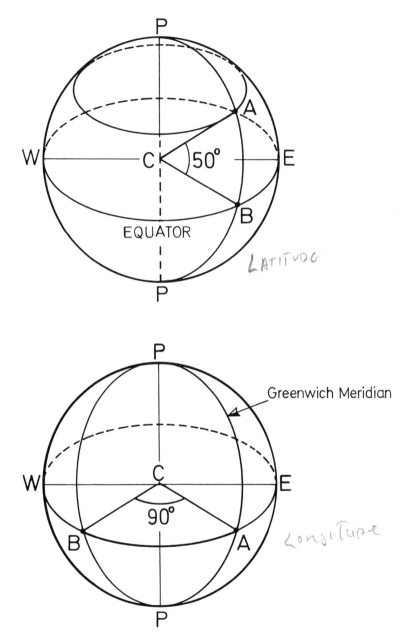

of the earth and its meridian and the Greenwich Meridian which has a value of zero. Longitude is always measured west or east from the Greenwich Meridian. The angle is measured at the centre of the earth in the plane of the Equator.

In the bottom diagram, P represents the poles, WE the equator, PAP the Greenwich Meridian, B a place on the surface of the earth, AB the longitude of B from A and ACB the angle at the centre of the earth representing the longitude.

Meridians are great circles which encompass the Earth through the poles. A line of longitude is a meridian measured in degrees, minutes and seconds from the Greenwich meridian.

Difference of Latitude and Longitude

Difference of latitude is always called Dlat and is measured by the angular difference between two places. If both places are in the same hemisphere the difference is subtracted to get the value of D lat. If the places are in different hemispheres the difference is added to get D lat. **Example**: Find the difference in latitude between London and Gibraltar

Latitude of London	51° 30' North
Latitude of Gibraltar	36° 07' North
D Lat	15° 23' or 923' of latitude

For a place in the Southern Hemisphere the latitude has to be added:

London	51° 30' North
Cape Town	33° 56' South
D Lat	85° 26' or a D Lat of 5156' of latitude

Difference of longitude is measured in the same way. If both places have a westerly longitude then the D long is obtained by subtracting the smaller longitude from the greater, but if one longitude is east and the other is west, then the longitudes are added to obtain D long. Of course if you are in a longitude greater than 90 east or west then the longitude has to be subtracted from 180 degrees to get the D long.

Nautical Mile and Cable

As all the meridians of longitude converge towards the poles the linear distance of a degree of longitude varies depending upon the latitude, so therefore cannot be taken as a measurement of mileage on the earth's surface. To simplify measurement one minute of the latitude scale is taken to represent a nautical or sea mile. The nautical mile is equivalent to one minute of arc along a meridian, but as this varies from about 6,108 ft at the poles to about 6,046 feet at the equator the mean is taken as the unit of measurement. This is 6,080 feet which is its value at about latitude 48 degrees.

It is essential to measure mileage from the latitude scale on the chart from which you are working adjacent to your approximate position. This is due to the distortion caused by representing a sphere on a flat surface. The term cable is traditionally used to refer to tenths of a nautical mile and is equivalent to 608 feet or roughly 200 yards or 100 fathoms. Nowadays it is usual to use decimals to indicate the fractions of a mile (e.g. 24.2 miles)

1 fathom ≈ 2 yards

The Knot *≈ s || ool*

The term knot is derived from the old method of finding a vessel's speed by streaming astern a knotted line. It is a measure of speed, not of distance and one knot is one nautical mile per hour. Because the nautical mile is longer than the land mile one knot is faster than one m.p.h. 10 knots equals about 11.5 miles per hour on land.

Chart knowledge

The main publishers of charts are the Admiralty, but there are two commercial publishers of charts for popular sailing areas, Stanfords and Imray. It is advisable to carry harbour charts of ports you intend to visit, larger scale coastal charts of your cruising area, and a smaller scale chart of the general area (for instance, a chart of the whole English Channel if you are intending a crossing).

Charts must be brought up to date before leaving, either from Admiralty Notices to Mariners (special quarterly edition for yachtsmen) or by a chart agent. Always store in a dry place and flat if possible. If you have to use them in the cockpit employ a plastic wallet. Note date of last correction when you buy a new chart and make new corrections in mauve indelible ink.

Stanford and Imray charts are published mainly for small boat navigation. They are intended to be simpler, are coloured and have course lines and distances marked on them and sometimes with harbour information on reverse side. The Admiralty publish practice charts for navigation students. These are clearly marked as such and in no circumstance should ever be used for navigation.

A wealth of information is obtainable from Admiralty charts and includes:

Depth in metres or fathoms (important to check which in corner of chart before using). This given both as spot depths and contour lines. Navigational aids such as buoys, lighthouses, daymarks, conspicuous objects.
Geographical features like headlands, creeks, harbours and estuaries.
Hazards and dangers such as reefs, rocks, sandbanks, and wrecks.
Tidal stream information and magnetic variation.

Chart symbols and conventional signs must be studied and the more common ones instantly recognised. Admiralty Chart No. 5011 (which is in fact a booklet) contains them all and will repay study.

Other publications

Several other publications are useful to the navigator. One is essential and that is a current nautical almanac with tide tables for the year and other tidal information. There is an Admiralty Nautical Almanac, but perhaps the most useful to yachtsmen is Reed's which also contains a mass of other information including list of lighthouses, pilotage and harbour entrance information, radio signals, etc.

Also useful to carry are

Tidal atlases
Admiralty pilot books
Commercially published yachtsmens pilot books

(the latter are of more relevance to the average yacht voyage, giving details of harbours and anchorages, but the relevant Admiralty pilot for the area should be consulted if no yachting publications are produced for the area or if you find yourself skippering a large yacht)

Dead Reckoning

The dead reckoning position, commonly known as the DR position, is found by using only two factors – course and speed. It is the position you reckon the vessel might be in after steering a course from the last known certain position and having covered a certain distance which may have been measured on the log. No other influences are taken into account. Quite often it is surprising how accurate the DR position is, particularly if the steering has been good and the speed of the vessel accurately recorded.

It is worth keeping the DR position plotted throughout the passage so that you know at least where you ought to be at any time. Ideally it should be plotted at hourly intervals on the chart. One advantage is that you then know approximately when you are likely to see a lighthouse or pick up a particular point of land, or whatever land or seamark you are relying on as a key point in your navigation. It also gives your crew confidence if they can see where they should be on the chart. More importantly however it gives you an approximate position if the onset of bad weather prevents you obtaining a fix.

The diagram shows a typical DR plotted along a course line with the log reading showing the distance run marked in.

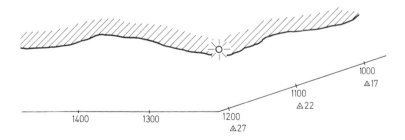

One way of checking the accuracy of a DR position is by comparing the soundings on the chart at the DR position with the reading you are getting on the echo sounder. This is a useful dodge in bad visibility.

It cannot be emphasised enough that keeping a regular DR plot going will help your basic coastal and deep sea navigation. With some yachts now carrying electronic navigational systems on board it may be considered perhaps that dead reckoning is not relevant, but the prudent navigator will continue to plot it on the chart.

The Estimated Position

The estimated position is the DR position with the effect of tidal stream or current and leeway taken into account. If you know the set and rate of the current you can plot this at the end of the DR position thus giving an estimated position or EP. The addition of leeway will make the estimated position of the vessel more accurate. The allowance for leeway will of necessity be an approximation, but the more you know your own vessel, or the vessel you are sailing, then the more accurately you will be able to judge.

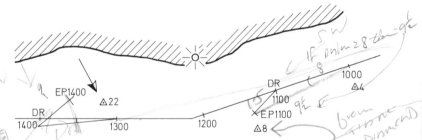

In the example here, from the DR at 1100 the tide was setting SW at 1.5 knots so this has been plotted from the DR position at 1100 to give an EP at 1100. In this case no leeway has been allowed. At 1300 with the wind from the NW 5 degrees of leeway has been allowed and the tidal stream has been setting NE at one knot, so a new position is found at 1400 which is different to the 1400 DR position.

When working out an EP leeway should be applied first and tidal set last. The estimated angle of leeway is measured from the DR course line (see angle A in diagram below) and this new line is known as the wake course. The distance run is marked off along the

14

wake course and from this point the direction of the tidal set is plotted to give a final EP which is then marked with a small triangle with the time and log reading beside it. There is no reason why an EP should not be plotted at hourly intervals instead of a DR, except that in practice constant small adjustments for leeway and tidal set, which may be altering frequently, can become confusing. It is probably better to keep the DR hourly and an EP at four hourly intervals, using a mean of the tidal stream and an average of the leeway over that period.

Of course a sailing yacht is very often not sailing a straight line along the course to be made good, but a DR may still be kept when tacking by plotting the heading of each tack and recording the distance run at the end of each tack.

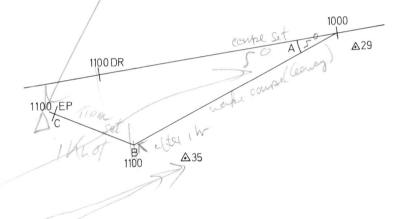

Questions

1 Write down the positions of Portland Bill, St Catherine's Point and Start Point.
2 Why can't you measure distance from the longitude scale?
3 How long is a nautical mile?
4 What criteria are necessary for plotting a DR position?
5 What criteria are necessary for plotting an estimated position?
6 When should you apply leeway to the course to obtain the estimated position?

2
POSITION LINES

A bearing plotted on the chart is a position line and a first step towards ascertaining your position accurately. A single position line can tell you only that you are somewhere on that line. It must be combined with other bearings or other information to tell you exactly where you are.

Position lines can be obtained from the following sources:

a compass bearing on a fixed identified object shown on the chart.
radio bearing
using a sextant
soundings
transits

Two or more position lines obtained by bearings of different objects constitute a **fix** which is a more or less accurate portrayal of where the vessel is on the chart.

16

The Transferred Position Line

This is a method of using a single position line to obtain a fix of the actual position. It is more commonly known as a running fix and there are several variants of the method which are described in the chapter on position fixing. It is useful when only one object is in view for the taking of bearings.

Radio bearings , *ie Know the Position of Radio Beacon*

Bearings of a radio beacon taken with radio direction finding navigation instruments can also be plotted on the chart as position lines. If only one is obtainable it might be combined with a visual bearing to provide a fix.

Sextant

Although the sextant is associated with ocean navigation it can be used effectively on more modest voyages. With an object in sight it can be used to give a very accurate fix as described later. Away from the coast with a good clear horizon it can also be used to obtain a position line. This in fact is just what the deep-sea navigator is doing when he shoots the sun at noon, because what he finds is the latitude which is in effect a position line.

When the sun reaches its maximum altitude during the day, around about noon, (it can be twenty minutes either side) then a sextant altitude taken then of the sun can produce a position line which will be a latitude. The bearing of the sun at noon will be due south if you are anywhere north of 24° N and as the position line will always lie at right angles to the bearing of the sun it must run in an east-west direction, thus giving a latitude.

If the lower limb of the sun is brought down to the observer's horizon and the angle on the sextant read, then to obtain a latitude or east and west position line we must refer to the **zenith**, the point directly overhead of the observer. To obtain this angle we subtract our sextant reading from 90 degrees. We have now to compare this angle with the celestial latitude of the sun which is called declination. This value is found in nautical almanacs for the time and day in question and as it varies from year to year the correct Nautical

17

Almanac for the year must be used. You will find that the sun's declination varies each day and each hour, but on June 22 and December 21 it reaches a maximum northerly and southerly declination (about 23.5° N in June and 23.5° S in December).

When comparing the declination with the sextant angle there is a simple rule. The sun will always be bearing south if you are north of 23½ degrees north latitude, or if you are in the southern hemisphere then the sun would always be bearing north if you were south of 23½ degrees south latitude.

The rule states that if the bearing of the sun and the declination have the same name, i.e., are both south (or both north) then to get the latitude you add the result of 90 minus sextant altitude to the declination. If the bearing of the sun is south and the declination is north then you subtract the smaller from the greater to get the latitude. This is all very well if we were using the angle of the sextant directly without subtracting from 90, but because we use the angle from directly above us (the zenith) to the sun we have to reverse the bearing of the sun.

For example, if the sun is actually bearing due south, then the name we use in our calculation will be north. If the sun is bearing north then we call it south. This may sound confusing, but in reality if you know your DR latitude you should make no mistake.

Example Vessel in DR position 50° 20′N 6° 42′W observes the sun at noon on June 1. The sextant gives an altitude of 61° 34′ bearing south.

Sextant altitude	61° 34′ bearing south.
Total correction	+ 12′
Subtract from 90	61° 46′
	90° 00′ reverse bearing to
	28° 14′N
Sun's declination	22° 01′N
Latitude	50° 15′N

The sun's total correction is a table allowing for small errors and is to be found in the nautical almanacs. It allows for your height of eye above sea level, refraction, the dip of the sea horizon and parallax. When using the sun for observation the total correction is always additive. So in celestial navigation the position line always runs at right angles to the bearing of the object being used whether it is the sun, stars or planets.

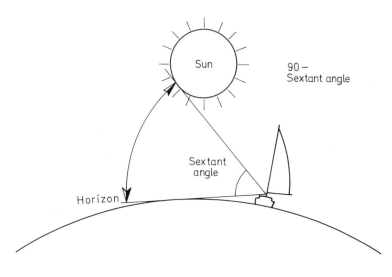

90 –
Sextant angle

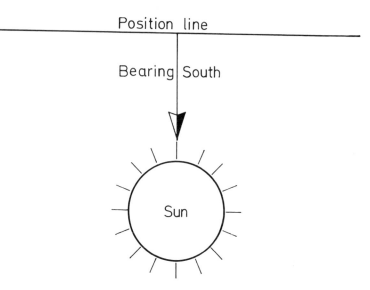

Soundings

In the absence of any other method of obtaining a position line (say in prolonged bad visibility) it is possible to obtain one by keeping the echo sounder (or lead line) going and comparing the depths found with the soundings on the chart in the region of your supposed course line. If you can do this the course line steered then in effect becomes the position line. Calculation will have to be made for the state of the tide to reduce the depths found to soundings (see tide chapter). Combined with one other position line found by other means this may be a useful dodge at times.

Transits

A transit is a line drawn through two fixed objects marked on the chart and projected seawards. A good navigator looks out for transit opportunities and makes use of them. Suppose you can see on the shore a lighthouse and near to it a church spire, both of which are shown on the chart. Watch for them coming into line, then plot the line through them and you will have a perfect position line because it has not been subject to any compass error or human error in taking a bearing. Two transits are unlikely to come up at the same time to give a fix, but one combined with a position line from any other source is going to give an accurate fix.

[handwritten margin note: ADVANTAGE OF TRANSIT LINES MARKED ON MAPS.]

Questions
[handwritten: com pass bearings, radio, soundings, transits, sextant]
1 Give some ways in which a position line may be obtained.
2 How can a position line be obtained from the sun?
3 What can you deduce from a position line? *[handwritten: on that line so member]*
4 What constitutes a fix? *[handwritten: Two or more lines crossing]*
5 Why is a transit reliable? *[handwritten: free of compass errors]*

3

THE MAGNETIC COMPASS

From very early times a suspended iron bar had been used to point in the direction of north to help man find his way at sea and by the 12th century sailors were using a pivoted needle very much like those of cheap pocket compasses to-day. Most modern compasses in small boats are of a type with a rotating card floating in a fluid filled bowl. This makes them much steadier and more accurate than a pivoting needle. They were the result of a mid 19th century development. As they are magnetic they point to magnetic north, unlike the electric gyroscopic compasses employed to-day in big ships which give a reading of true north.

Variation

The difference between true and magnetic north is known as **variation** and is an essential factor to be taken into account in navigation. The magnetic north and south poles move, causing a continual shift in the earth's magnetic field. As a result compass variation is always changing and has widely different values at different places.

At the moment the magnetic north pole lies somewhere in the Hudson Bay area. Magnetic variation in the English Channel is at present around 6 degrees west of true north and is decreasing by about 8 minutes annually. Much greater values will be found in other places. The Admiralty produces a special chart showing magnetic variation for anywhere in the world, places of equal variation being joined by lines called isogenic lines. It should rarely be necessary to consult one of these since all charts have a compass rose which shows the amount of variation from true north at one or more places. This also notes by how much variation is increasing or decreasing annually, so if the date of the chart's publication is noted (always found in one of the corners) the exact variation at the time of using can be worked out. On the average yachtsman's cruising chart it is unlikely that there will be a calculable difference in variation between one part of it and another. On a small scale, long distance chart there will be appreciable differences, but the rule is always to use the compass rose nearest to one's present position.

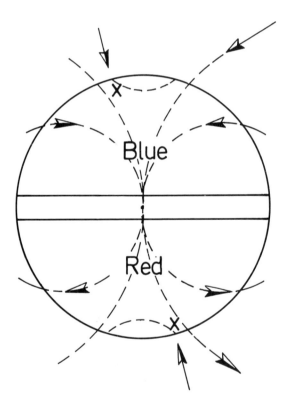

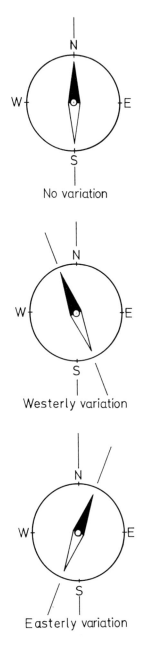

No variation

Westerly variation

Easterly variation

Deviation

It follows that magnetic compasses can be subject to any ferrous influence which will further deflect them from a true reading. A steel hull is itself likely to cause substantial deviation. There should be little or none from wood and plastic hulls, but such yachts are not immune from deviation because other influences may be at work such as:

the engine, (especially if near the compass),

the mast,

electric wiring,

any metal fitting with a ferric content,

heeling (deviation may be caused or change if the vessel is heeled for a long time on one heading),

laying up (deviation in a vessel may change if laid up a long time in one position because the hull or fittings become polarised),

fitting out (changes may also occur because gear has been stowed differently after a fit-out, or new equipment has been installed).

electronic equipment (many items contain small magnets) .

All the above are fixed causes of deviation which will be calculated when **swinging the compass** (see section below), but beware of creating other compass errors caused by putting moveable metal objects down near the compass or the helmsman wearing a knife, etc. It is also worth starting the engine, pumps and generators, etc to observe whether these deflect the compass differently when running.

Other Compass Effects

Some other factors influence the compass from time to time. The yacht skipper should be aware of them and when necessary navigate with caution.

Magnetic storms (including thunder and lightning) can temporarily disturb the compass, though this will probably be short lived.

Local magnetic anomalies where the compass appears to read very erratically exist in some parts of the world. They are usually marked with a cautionary note on the charts. One occurs off the West coast of Scotland. There is one off West Australia where a change in variation from 56 E to 26 W in the space of 200 yards is said to have been observed.

Magnetic dip is a downward pull on the needle caused by the attraction of the magnetic equator, which only approximately follows the geographical equator. Manufacturers compensate for this so there is no need for navigators to worry about it.

Finding The Deviation

As we have seen the amount of variation affecting a compass can be found by looking at the chart. There is no source of reference for deviation. It is individual to every vessel and further complicated by the fact that it changes with the course steered. In other words there may be one amount of deviation when the yacht is heading north and a quite different amount when she is sailing west. It is essential for the navigator to know what the deviation is for each different heading so that allowances can be made for it and this is done by the process known as swinging the compass.

There are various methods of doing this but perhaps the simplest is to anchor and tow the stern of the vessel round with the dinghy while taking a series of bearings of objects ashore with a hand bearing compass, which is used well away from any magnetic influences. These bearings are compared with the reading of the steering compass and the differences noted in graph form to draw up a deviation card like that illustrated. If one or more of the bearings used can be a transit it will help to ensure the accuracy of the operation. An alternative is to have a steady helmsman steer the vessel on different headings while someone takes bearings and compares the steering compass readings. Whichever method is used the readings must be taken all round the compass at intervals of 45 degrees.

Deviation cards should be re-worked about once a year and after major re-fits. A professional compass adjuster can be employed and it may be wise to consult one if the deviation on any headings appears excessive, say more than four degrees. Large amounts of deviation can be reduced by the siting of correcting pieces of iron (Flinders bars), but this is a professional job.

westerly Easterly

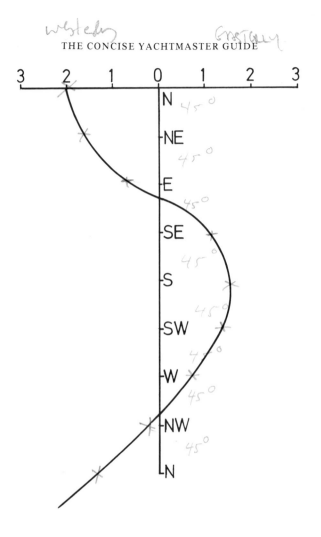

Typical deviation chart

Steering and Hand Bearing Compasses

The steering compass is the main compass of the vessel. It needs to be sited where the helmsman can most easily see it and if possible where he can see it from directly behind, so that any parralex error is avoided in looking at it. It also needs to be where it will be least subject to deviation from the kind of influences listed above.

In larger yachts the compass is mounted on a pedestal called a binnacle which puts it at a convenient height for the helmsman, puts it high enough to have an all round view of the horizon so that it can be used if necessary for bearings and can house the deviation correcting bars mentioned above. Binnacles also have covers which house a light to illuminate the card for night sailing while at the same time protecting from glare. Smaller yachts without room for a binnacle often have to have the steering compass fixed on the cockpit bulkhead from which it can be unshipped when not in use. Whatever sort of compass is used must be fitted in gimbals so that it is not made ineffective (unable to swing) by the rolling of the ship.

All modern compasses are notated in degrees from 0 (north) through 90 (east), 180 (south) and 270 (west) round to 359. To avoid possible errors all degrees are given in three digits, even for single and two digit numbers. Thus a course of 10 degrees would be written as 010 degrees and passed to the helmsman verbally as 'zero one zero'. A bearing of 45 degrees would be recorded in the log as 045 and spoken as 'zero four five'.

Older yachts may be fitted with the traditional compass noted in 'points', each point being named and equivalent to 11 1/4 degrees. Therefore 32 points make up the complete circle. The four key directions (north south, east and west) are known as **cardinal** points and the four intermediate ones (north east, south east, south west and north west) as **half cardinals**. At one time it was the first task of fledgeling sailors to learn to 'box the compass', that is to be able to recite without hesitation all 32 points of the compass in correct order. Although the modern yachtsman may rarely find himself sailing with a points compass, and although most references to bearings and courses on charts and elsewhere are now made in degrees, there is a lot to be said for becoming familiar with the names of the compass points. Wind directions, for instance, are always given from a point of the compass in weather forecasts and gale warnings, and pilot books may have been written some time ago and still give bearings, courses, or tidal stream directions in the old way.

The 32 points are:

N NbyE NNE NEbyN NE NEbyE ENE EbyN E EbyS ESE

SEbyE SE SEbyS SSE SbyE S SbyW SSW SWbyS SW SWbyW

WSW WbyS W WbyN WNW NWbyW NW NWbyN NNW NbyW

Many modern compasses marked in degrees do show on the card the cardinal and sometimes the half cardinal points as well. Some omit the final 0 from degree numbers in order to have clear, uncluttered lettering which is more easily read. On these compasses 280 degrees would appear as 28 and 20 degrees as 2.

A line is usually etched on the fixed outer rim of the compass, or on its glass or perspex cover. This is the **lubber line** and when the compass is fixed must line up with the fore and after line of the vessel. To the helmsman this represents the ship's head and helps the steering of an accurate course.

Hand Bearing Compass

It is not possible to take accurate bearings with most yacht compasses as they can rarely be mounted high enough to have an uninterupted all round view of the horizon. It is not possible to be accurate just squinting along them anyway. Big ship compasses are usually fitted with a device with a special ring which can be lined up on a target while the bearing is read. A device sometimes used if the steering compass is not in a suitable position is a **pelorus**. This is not a compass, but a mounted flat disc marked out with the compass gradations and equipped with sights. The pelorus is set so that the course being steered by the helmsman is pointing to the bows, so that it is in effect giving the same reading as the steering compass. Bearings are then taken with it, using the sights.

For the majority of yacht skippers the simple hand held bearing compass is more convenient, though having the disadvantage, which the pelorus does not, of being subjected to the same magnetic influences as the steering compass. All hand bearing compasses have a means of sighting and many are prismatic to magnify the figures for clarity. Some also incorporate batteries for night use. So far as possible they must be used away from deviating influences. The mast, if steel, is perhaps the biggest influence in this case. The deviation of the hand bearing compass should be noted at the same time as the steering compass is swung. It also has to be remembered that a bearing compass reading will be magnetic. When being laid off on the chart bearings must be laid off against the magnetic rose or first converted to true.

Allowing For Variation and Deviation

All courses laid off on the chart should be true, not compass. The letter T should be placed against them thus: 270 (T). The skipper or navigator must convert these to a compass course for the helmsman to steer and all compass bearings should be converted to true. In order to do this it is necessary to take into account both the variation and deviation. The sum of the two is known as **compass error**.

If the variation and the deviation are both to the same side (i.e. both west or both east) add them both together to find the compass error. If they are on opposite sides (i.e. one west, one east) then take the smaller one away from the bigger one. Examples Variation 6 W + deviation 3 W = compass error 9 W Variation 6 W − deviation 3 E = compass error 3 W To convert a true course to a compass course move to the left on the compass rose (in other words subtract it) if the error is easterly. If the error is westerly move to the right, or add it. Thus: True course 270. Compass error 5 E. Course to steer 265 True course 270. Compass error 5 W. Course to steer 275

Of course exactly the reverse applies converting compass bearings to true.

The following nemomics may be helpful
TELC = True East Left Compass
CERT = Compass East Right True

Questions

1 Define magnetic variation.
2 Give three causes of magnetic deviation.
3 What is meant by swinging the compass?
4 You have variation of 10° W and deviation of 2° W.
5 You have variation of 10° W and deviation of 3° E what is the compass error?
6 You wish to sail a true course of 180° and the compass error is 5° W. What compass course will you steer?
7 You wish to sail a true course of 65° and the compass error is 3° E. What compass course will you steer?

4
on Bearings
rings on the chart
POSITION FIXING

Speed + course from last known point
Bearing / Time.

It is necessary to obtain a fix of the yacht's position at sea at intervals and not to rely on DR and EP. Radio and electronic methods of doing this are now widely available, but, however well provided with modern aids, a qualified yacht skipper must be capable of using all traditional visual methods to check his position during the course of every passage.

A fix should be plotted on the chart, marked with a small circle and the time against it. Visual position fixing relies on the accuracy of bearings taken by the navigator Such accuracy is difficult to achieve in a small boat moving in a seaway and so is the accuracy of the bearings plotted on the chart in the confined space of a rolling cabin. Frequent practice is therefore desirable, even when the fixes may not be strictly needed.

Crossed Bearings

This is the simplest and most frequently used small boat method. As we have seen a bearing on one object gives a position line showing that the vessel is somewhere on that line. Bearings on two different objects will provide two position lines. If these are plotted on the chart the point at which they intersect should be the fixed position of the vessel. The most reliable fix is obtained by choosing two objects whose bearings will as near as possible be at right angles to each other, though this is not often possible. In any event they should be at a good wide angle apart, not too close together, nor yet so far apart that they make an angle closer to 180 degrees.

In the example shown the two fixes have been taken with a good angle, giving a reliable position. Bearings should be taken as quickly as possible after each other and noted down. Do not stop to plot one on the chart before you take the other or the first one will have changed in the meantime. If one bearing is on the beam, take that last as it will alter more quickly than one ahead or astern. It is common practice to take three bearings if three objects are in view. Given the difficulty of taking accurate bearings it is unlikely that all three will cross neatly at one point. Usually they produce a triangle called a **cocked hat**. If this is only small the position of the fix may be safely assumed somewhere inside the cocked hat. If it is large it is better to re-take the bearings and try again. If circumstances don't permit this and you are worried about the size of the cocked hat look on the chart for the nearest point of danger (rocks, shoals, etc) and put your position down in the nearest point in the cocked hat to that danger. If you are sailing the nearest point of danger may not be the hazard closest by distance, but one which happens to be to leeward of you.

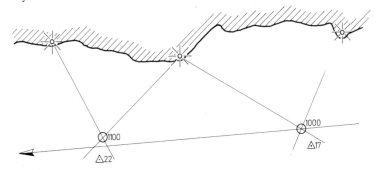

These two fixes have been taken at a good angle, so giving a more reliable fix

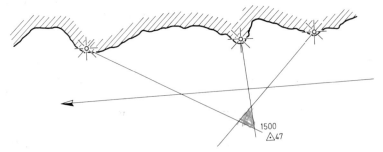

Typical 'cocked hat' produced by three bearings

Bearing Objects

Objects chosen for bearings must be ones which are marked on the chart and which you can identify with certainty, with the aid of binoculars if necessary. Headlands are often used but require caution because it is very easy from seaward to mistake one for another and unless you have a profile view you cannot be certain you are sighting the bearing compass on the end point of land. Tall structures like lighthouses, radio masts, beacons, daymarks, churches etc make the best objects. Look at the chart in advance to see which ones are likely to come into view and watch out for them. You should know from your DR when to expect to sight them.

Buoys at sea are also possible objects but also need treating with reservation. Unless it is a named buoy you cannot be certain you are identifying the right one. If you are near enough to read the name you have a good check of your whereabouts anyway. Buoys may also have been removed for servicing or have dragged out of position during a storm, though these circumstances are rare.

Running Fix

Frequently it happens that only one object suitable for a bearing is in view, providing only a single position line. By using the vessel's own course and speed it is possible to get a position called a running fix, or a transferred position line. This method has limited accuracy as it depends upon a straight course being steered and an accurate knowledge of the vessel's speed. It must also include the slightly doubtful knowledge about the set and rate of the tidal current. Nevertheless a running fix is better than nothing at all.

The first example is of a running fix with no current being allowed for. Assume you are on your course line. Taking a bearing of the lighthouse and lay it off on the chart so that it cuts the course line at 1000hrs. After one hour take another bearing of the same lighthouse and lay it off on the chart. Read the log at 1000 and 1100 and lay off the distance travelled along the course line. If it coincides with the 1100 bearing then you are on or near the course line, but if it does not then transfer the first bearing (pecked line in diagram) with the parallel rules and draw it through the place on the course line where your speed is marked for one hour. Where this first transferred bearing cuts the second bearing is the probable position of the vessel.

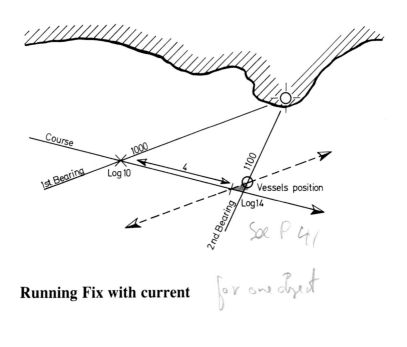

Running Fix with current

for one object

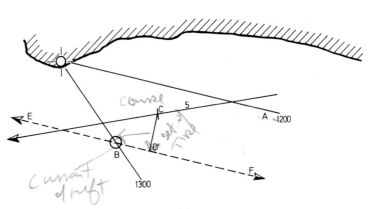

First find the rate and direction of the current from the chart or tidal atlas. At the end of the distance run between the bearings plot the direction of the current and parallel through that point at the end of the current, and where the first bearing cuts the second bearing will be the probable position of the vessel.

A is the first bearing, B is the second bearing. The vessel's speed of 5 knots from A to C. Line CD is the set and rate of the current. Pecked line EF is the first bearing transferred to the point D and where it cuts the second bearing B is the vessel's probable position.

Four Point Bearing

This is a simple mathematical exercise which uses the fact that in an isosceles triangle the two base angles are equal and the two adjacent sides are equal in length. It is another form of fix for use when only one object for a bearing is in view. In this case instead of waiting until a certain period of time has elapsed the bearings are taken at intervals which are mathematically suitable.

For example, if the course is 270 then to get a four point bearing we need to take the bearing of the lighthouse when it is bearing 45 degrees on the bow (i.e. 315). To complete the exercise we take another bearing when the lighthouse is abeam (i.e. at 90 degrees to our course), in this case when it is bearing 000. Then the distance

35

run between the bearings will be automatically the distance the vessel is from the lighthouse, and can be measured off along the second position line with the dividers.

The four point bearing method is so called because the difference between the two bearings is four compass points or 45°. It used to be a very common way of navigating round a coastline before the use of radar and can still be very useful for the yacht skipper as a way of knowing when to alter course round a headland.

Doubling the angle on the bow

Another form of running fix is to take a bearing of an object say at 25 degrees on the bow and then a second bearing when the bearing of the same object is 50 degrees on the bow. Any two figures which double the angle will do. The distance run on the log between these two bearings will be the distance off the object at the time of the second bearing.

This means again waiting until the bearing is at a certain angle before plotting, can be completed but it has the advantage of giving you an instant distance off the object, which could be useful knowledge if for instance it is a headland with offlying rocks.

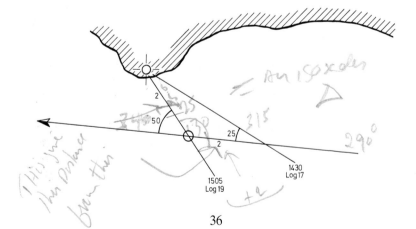

Position from a line of soundings

This was a method used by sailing vessels many years ago when approaching land. By using the speed of the vessel and the course being steered regular soundings are taken at say half an hour intervals and by careful consideration of the chart the vessel's position may be obtained. The method is not very accurate, but can be useful if there is nothing else to obtain a position from.

It is best to plot the sounding on a piece of tracing paper with the vessel's course drawn on and try to fit the tracing paper over the chart where it gives the best similarity of soundings.

The log distance must be read at the same time as the sounding to get the best position.

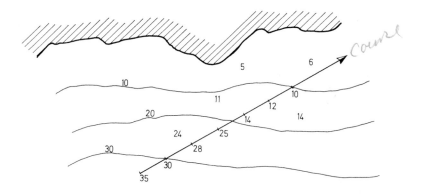

Vertical Sextant Angle

A good position may be obtained by taking a compass bearing of a lighthouse and at the same time using the sextant to take a vertical sextant angle which will give a distance off the lighthouse by using the tables in the nautical almanacs.

As long as you know the height of the object, and in the case of the lighthouse it is always given, then by bringing the top of the lighthouse down to the sea level and reading off the angle on the sextant you will obtain a distance off the lighthouse. This coupled with the visual bearing will give a good position.

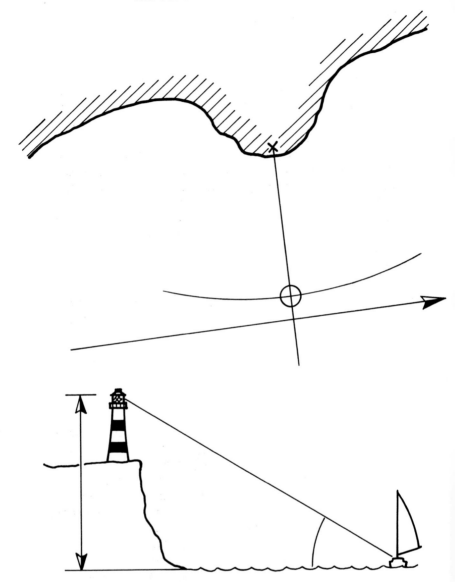

Height of lighthouse found with a sextant can be used to determine distance off. This plus a bearing gives a good position

Rising and dipping bearings

A position can be found approximately when a lighthouse is seen to rise above the horizon or dip below the horizon. If a bearing is taken at the same time then a position can be obtained. The accuracy is not very great, but should be within one or two miles. You need a clear horizon with good visibility to be able to use this method. There are tables in the nautical almanacs using the height of the lighthouse and your height of eye above sea level which will then give you the rising or dipping distance. A rising light is probably easier to obtain as you are looking forward and is usually more relevant anyway than a dipping distance astern of you. It is comforting to be able to do this exercise approaching a strange coast at night. First of all on a clear night you will see the loom of the light followed by the light itself flashing on the horizon.

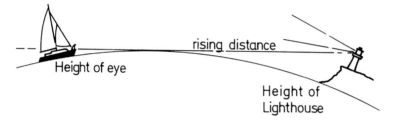

Horizontal Sextant Angle

The sextant can be used to obtain a fix by a method known as horizontal angle fixing. The position obtained tends to be more accurate than a compass bearing because the sextant can be read more accurately than the compass and it is independent of any compass errors. However it does take a little time to work out and you do need three visual objects. To obtain a position the sextant must be held horizontally and the angle measured between two objects on the coast. The angle is then measured between the second object and the third. To plot on the chart you use a piece of tracing paper with the angles drawn with the lines going to the three objects and fitting them where they should be, and by pressing a small hole through the paper you can mark on the chart the vessel's position.

39

An instrument called a station pointer can be used for this problem. It consists of a graduated circle with three arms two of which can be moved to the angles required. A small hole in the middle of the plastic circle enables the mariner to plot the vessel's position.

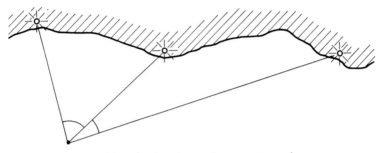

Position by horizontal sextant angle

A Mixture of Position Lines

It is possible to use a mixture of position lines from different sources. It may be that you can take one visual bearing of a lighthouse and combine this with a radio bearing. Add to this a sounding and you will probably have a reliable idea of your position. The question of radio fixes is dealt with in the chapter on radio aids to navigation.

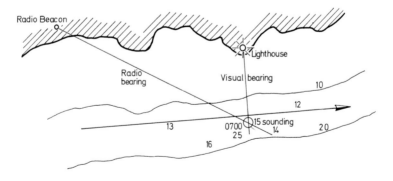

You can also get a fix from single bearings of different lighthouses at different times with the vessel's speed and course being allowed for in between and by transferring the first bearing on to the second bearing. This is another variation on the running fix.

If the vessel takes a bearing at 1000 and the log reads 12 then at 1200 takes another bearing of a different lighthouse with the log reading 20, then by transferring the first bearing through the end of the logged distance will give a position at 1200. There is no reason why any combination of ideas for obtaining a position should not be used.

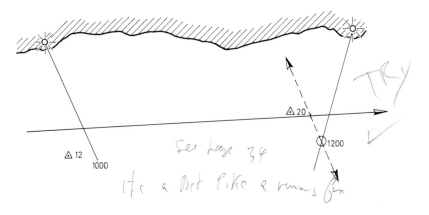

△ 20

△ 12
1000

1200

See page 34

It's a fix like a running fix

TRY

Questions *three bearing not neatly together But fairly a small △*

1 What is meant by a 'cocked hat'
2 How can a position be obtained with a sextant with only a lighthouse in view? *?*
3 Name three other methods of obtaining a fix with only one object in sight *Running fix for head Bearing, Powell angle a Bar*
4 What limitations have buoys as navigational aids? *off station, Identification*
5 What are rising and dipping bearings? *Bearing — Bearing of a Lighthouse just appearing or dipping over Horizon.*

41

5

TIDES

The state of the tide makes a considerable difference to the depth of water found in any place around coasts and an understanding of them is essential to safe navigation. The gravitational pull of the sun and moon (mainly the moon because although a smaller mass it is nearer to the earth) acts upon every body of water on the earth. There are unimaginably tiny tides on a garden pond. In European waters we are used to tides which are semi-diurnal, or occurring in a twice daily cycle giving two high waters and two low waters. This is not so in all parts of the globe.

Big range of Hi+Low   New + full moon

Springs and Neaps

Anyone using the sea quickly becomes familiar with references to two types of tide – spring tides and neap tides, or just springs and neaps for short.

Spring tides are greater in range. The word itself from ancient Norse means 'big' and has nothing to do with the season of the year. When there are spring tides the high tide will be higher than at other times and the low tide will fall lower. This is a fact of considerable importance for those frequenting drying harbours, shallow estuaries and so forth. Spring tides occur at the new moon when the moon and sun are pulling in the same direction and also (oddly it may seem) at the full moon when sun and moon are at opposite sides of the earth. *Less range of High+Low*

Neap tides occur when sun and moon are at right angles. Because they are exerting less pull in this position the tidal range is smaller. High water during neaps is lower than at springs, but also low water does not fall so far.

The movement from neaps to springs and back is not of course a jump, but a gradual curve and the cycle is a fortnightly one in line with the lunar month. Spring tides will reach their highest at about new and full moon (actually in Northern Europe approximately two days after) and then gradually become less each tide for the next week until the smallest neap range is reached. They then begin to build up again for a week until it is springs again. From neaps to springs the tides are said to be **making** and in the period from springs to neaps are said to be **taking off**.

As the heavenly bodies orbit elliptically they vary in distance from each other and this provides another factor in the gravitational influence. When the sun and moon are closest to the earth (perigee and perihelion) there is a higher than average range of spring tides and when they are furthest away (apogee and aphelion) we have less than average rise and fall in the spring tides. This influence is most marked around the equinoxes (March 21 and September 23) when we tend to have the biggest tides of the year.

Tidal Definitions

Yachtmaster candidates will already be aware of a number of other tidal expressions in everyday use at sea. It is important to be thoroughly familiar with those below.

Chart datum (CD) The plane or theoretical level from which the chartmakers calculate the depth of the sea bed. It is usually set at a point below which the tide seldom falls.

Soundings. The depth of water below chart datum as shown on the chart for all places permanently covered by the sea. This figure has to be added to the height of tide for that place and time taken from the tide tables. On up to date charts soundings are shown in metres, to one decimal point in shallower places. On older charts they are given in fathoms and feet. Before using a chart it is essential to note which, the information being always clearly stated in one corner.

Drying heights. Places periodically covered and uncovered by the tide are call drying heights. The heights above chart datum to which they are exposed are marked on the chart with a line beneath the figure to distinguish them from soundings. This figure must be subtracted from the tide height for the day in any calculations you are making.

Lowest Astronomical Tide (LAT) This is the lowest level of tide that is likely to occur in any predictable set of circumstances. The tide only rarely falls to this level, perhaps not as much as once a year, and will only fall below it if freak meteorological conditions combine with rare astronomical ones. By international agreement all the chart making organisations now fix their CD at or very close to LAT.

Mean Low Water Springs (MLWS) Average level of low water at spring tides. Older charts made before LAT came into use will have CD fixed near MLWS.

Mean High Water Springs (MHWS) Average level of high water at spring tides.

Mean High (or Low) Water Neaps (MHWN or MLWN) Average level of high or low waters respectively at neap tides.

Mean Level The average of the high and low water heights. The figure is a mean of the four above – MHWS, MLSW, MHWN and MLWN.

Tidal range The difference between any high water height and the preceeding or succeeding low water height.

Height of tide The height to which a particular tide will rise above chart datum in a particular place, as given in the tide table. It does not tell you the depth of water anywhere, but is a figure which enables you to calculate the depth, *using the CP figure + propn by the length of Tide for less Time.*

Duration of Mean Rise (DMR) The times of high tide advance by approximately 50 minutes each day, keeping pace with the lunar day. So the time between high tides is approximately 12 hours 25 minutes and the time between high and low water 6 hours 12 minutes. These times occur fairly predictably along open coasts so that we can rely on just over six hours flood followed by six hours ebb. In estuaries and other more complex coastal configurations however there may be considerable difference between the flood and ebb, one running for half an hour or more longer than the other. The average length of the flood, or duration of mean rise, is given with other tidal information in nautical almanacs.

Tide Tables

In almost any harbour information about the times of high water and the height for the day can be obtained either from local booklets published annually or from notices posted by harbourmasters, local authorities and yacht clubs. While this information may be sufficient for anyone day sailing in the immediate vicinity it will not suffice for anyone intending to make a voyage to other ports when it is good practice to have in advance tidal knowledge about the places to be visited. This is obtained from one of the nautical almanacs or from the Admiralty Tide Tables.

All these books are published each year with many pages of tide tables of different ports, giving high and low water for every day of the year and the height of tide. The ports chosen are known as the standard ports. In addition information is given about smaller or secondary ports, enabling you to work out the tide times and heights for yourself from the table for the nearest standard port.

Admiralty Tide Tables are in several volumes covering the world, volume one being for European waters from Iceland to the Mediterranean. The best known of nautical almanacs is Reed's which, in addition to the tide tables, contains a wealth of seamanship and navigational information. Originally published for professional shipmasters it has now been widely used by yachtsmen for many years. Others are Brown's, also long used in the merchant service, and Olsen's which caters particularly for fishermen. More recently has appeared the Macmillan Silk Cut Almanac specially for yachtsmen and containing a good deal of pilotage information about popular yachting areas. Familiarity with the use of the information in these publications is essential.

Remember that the tables are properly called tidal predictions. Times and heights can be affected by changes in barometric pressure, possibly at some far off spot in the ocean, making a difference of as much as a foot in height. Strong and sustained winds from one direction can have a similar effect. To ensure a comfortable anchorage or the safe passage of a yacht over shallow waters a margin of error should always be allowed after making tidal calculations. Use must always be made of a current nautical almanac. Guesses cannot be made from last year's.

Working Out Times and Heights of Tide *For Ports/Harbours*

The tables for standard ports give times of both high and low water. These are always given in Greenwich Mean Time. Conversion to the local zone time must be made in the relevant months. For most readers that will mean adding one hour for British Summer Time between the end of the March and the end of October. A reminder appears on most tide table pages, but it is easy to forget.

Alongside are given the heights. These show the actual depth above chart datum at high and low water respectively at a particular measuring point, usually near the harbour entrance. That figure can be added to the soundings on the chart to give a depth of water anywhere at high or low water (remembering to make a substraction in the case of drying heights shown with a line beneath). This information is essential if you want to know if you have clearance to enter a harbour which, for instance, has a sandbar at the entrance. The answer of course depends on the draught of your vessel (how far it is from the waterline to the bottom of the keel). If you are chartering a yacht or skippering somebody else's make sure you know the draught before you go anywhere.

Associated with each of the standard port tables is a table of **tidal differences**. This lists secondary ports in the area, showing how much earlier or later the tide will be there, and how much higher or lower. The calculations are simple but to reduce the possibility of errors the Admiralty issue sheets to do tidal calculations on. These make sure you do not leave out any vital step and many people find them helpful. Their reference number is NP204.

Example Find the times of High and Low water for Dover on May 1. Reading from the table reproduced the times of high and low water are High water 0826 and 2049 with heights of 6.0 and 6.3 metres. Low water 0327 and 1553 with heights of 1.2 and 1.2 metres. These times are GMT so for BST then you must add one hour to the times given.

If you wished to find the times and height of high water at Ramsgate for August 2 you would have to consult the tidal differences on Dover.

DOVER

HIGH & LOW WATER
1981 **G.M.T.** ADD 1 HOUR MARCH 22-OCTOBER 25 FOR B.S...

MAY

Day	Time h.min.	Ht. m.	Time h.min.	Ht. m.
1 F	0327	1.2	**16** 0447	1.2
	0826	6.0	0939	5.9
	1553	1.2	1706	1.3
	2049	6.3	2149	6.2
2 Sa	0424	0.8	**17** 0525	1.1
	0912	6.4	1013	6.1
	1647	0.9	1740	1.2
	2135	6.6	2226	6.3
3 Su	0516	0.6	**18** 0556	1.1
	0957	6.6	1048	6.2
	1736	0.7	1807	1.1
	2220	6.8	2302	6.4
4 M	0604	0.5	**19 Tu** 0624	1.0
	1044	6.8	1122	6.3
	1821	0.6	1838	1.0
	2306	6.9	2336	6.4

JUNE

Day	Time h.min.	Ht. m.	Time h.min.	Ht. m.
1 M	0444	0.8	**16** 0518	1.3
	0938	6.5	1024	6.1
	1705	0.9	1734	1.3
	2159	6.7	2237	6.2
2	0537	0.6	**17** 0554	1.1
	1028	6.6	1101	6.3
Tu	1757	0.7	**W** 1814	1.1
	2248	6.8	2312	6.3
3	0629	0.6	**18** 0634	1.0
	1120	6.7	1133	6.3
W	1848	0.7	**Th** 1853	1.0
	2339	6.8	2343	6.2
4	0721	0.6	**19** 0712	1.0
	1212	6.7	1205	6.3
Th	1938	0.6	**F** 1931	1.0
	—	—	—	—

JULY

Day	Time h.min.	Ht. m.	Time h.min.	Ht. m.
1	0520	0.9	**16** 0530	1.2
	1020	6.5	1037	6.2
W	1742	1.0	**Th** 1754	1.2
	2238	6.6	2247	6.2
2	0621	0.8	**17** 0614	1.1
	1112	6.6	1109	6.3
Th	1839	0.8	**F** 1836	1.1
	2330	6.6	2319	6.3
3	0716	0.8	**18** 0655	1.0
	1200	6.7	1143	6.5
F	1933	0.7	**Sa** 1917	1.0
	—	—	2354	6.3
4	0019	6.6	**19** 0733	1.0
	0806	0.8	1218	6.5
Sa	1243	6.6	**Su** 1954	0.9
	2022	0.7	—	—

AUGUST

Day	Time h.min.	Ht. m.	Time h.min.	Ht. m.
1	0713	0.9	**16** 0638	1.0
	1144	6.7	1118	6.6
Sa	1927	0.8	**Su** 1902	0.9
	—	—	2332	6.5
2	0004	6.6	**17** 0717	0.9
	0759	0.9	1156	6.7
Su	1224	6.7	**M** 1938	0.8
	2011	0.7	—	—
3	0043	6.5	**18** 0011	6.6
	0837	0.9	0749	0.9
M	1302	6.7	**Tu** 1235	6.8
	2050	0.8	2009	0.8
4	0123	6.4	**19** 0055	6.6
	0910	1.1	0819	0.9
Tu	1340	6.6	**W** 1317	6.7
	2124	1.0	2042	0.8

TIDAL DIFFERENCES ON DOVER

PLACE	MHW Tm. Diff. h. min.	MHW Ht. Diff. m.	MLW Tm. Diff. h. min.	MLW Ht. Diff. m.	HWS m.	HWN m.	CD m.	POSITION
Hastings	− 0 05	+ 0.6	− 0 30	0.0	9.0	7.3	1.5	Entrance
Rye (Apprs.)	0 00	+ 0.8	−	−	6.2	4.5	− 1.5	Bar near entrance
Dungeness	− 0 15	+ 1.2	− 0 15	+ 0.2	15.3	13.6	7.3	West Road Anche.
Folkestone	− 0 10	+ 0.4	− 0 10	0.0	5.5	3.1	− 1.6	Alongside Sth Quay
Dover	0 00	0.0	0 00	0.0	7.1	5.7	0.4	Entce. Granville Dock
Deal	+ 0 15	− 0.4	+ 0 05	0.0	10.1	9.0	4.0	Pier Head
Richborough	+ 0 15	− 1.0	−	−	2.8	1.7	− 0.9	Chan to
Ramsgate	+ 0 20	− 1.6	− 0 07	− 0.6	5.0	3.9	0.1	Entrance

Reproduced courtesy of Reed's Nautical Almanac

Depth of Water Calculations

It is often essential to know the depth of water at times between low and high water. Will you be able to anchor in some pleasant bay without going aground? With three hours to go to high water will it be safe for you to enter a harbour? The handiest method of doing is this by what is popularly known as the **Twelfths Rule**, based on the fact that the tide rises or falls one twelfth of its range in the first hour, two twelfths in the second hour, three twelfths in the third hour, three twelfths in the fourth hour, two twelfths in the fifth hour and one twelfth in the sixth hour. First you must know the range of the tide which is the difference between the high and low water depths in the tide table. If you are not near the standard port note the height difference for the nearest secondary port.

Example To find the height of the tide at 1230 BST at Dover on June 1. High water is at 1038 BST with a height of 6.5 m. The range is 5.6 m (The difference in height between high and low water). As it is 2 hrs after high water then the 1st hour is 1/12 of the range plus the 2nd hour which is 2/12 of the range, which makes it 3/12 of the range altogether 3/12 (or 1/4) of 5.6 = 1.4, so the height of the tide at 1230 BST will be 6.5 m – 1.4 m = 5.1 m.

Dover High water	0004	6.6	1224	6.7
Correction for Ramsgate	+20	−1.6	+20	−1.6
Ramsgate High water	0024	5.0	1244	5.1
Plus 1 hour for BST	0124		1344	

The twelfths rule is only an approximation. It assumes an even six hour ebb and flood and a symmetrical pattern of behaviour which is not the case everywhere. However, given the fact that no navigator will rely on tidal calculations which do not allow for a good margin of error the twelfths rule is perfectly safe for most yachtsmen to use most of the time.

A simplified version of it can also be used. This is as follows:
1 hour before or after high or low water the tide will rise or fall one twelfth of its range.
2 hours before or after it will rise or fall one quarter of its range.
3 hours before or after it will rise or fall half its range.

Tidal Curves

A more accurate method of finding depth of water at any particular time is with the use of Admiralty tidal curves, an example of which is reproduced here. It will be seen from the shape of this graph that the tide does not in fact behave in a completely symmetrical pattern and not all the curves look alike. The waters of the Solent particularly have very asymetrical curves. Note that the Spring Tide curve is marked with a continuous line and that the Neap curve is a pecked line.

The arguments used for the curve are along the bottom denoting hours before and after high water and down the middle called the factor. The ranges for both springs and neaps are given in the box at the side of the curve and the range can be found from the tide tables, so you can find out whether the spring curve or the neap curve should be used. If it lies between the two then some interpolation is needed. The factor is a multiplier which, when it is applied to the range of the tide, gives the rise of tide. The rise of tide is equal to factor times the range.

Example Find the height of the tide at Bembridge on July 1 at 1700 BST. Using the left hand side of the graph:
1 Mark the predicted height of High Water along the top line.
   Portsmouth HW 1542   4.2   Portsmouth LW   2019   1.6
   Correction for Bembridge –
              0 00   –1.5   Bembridge   + 10   – 1.0
   Bembridge HW   1542   2.7   Bembridge LW   2029   0.6
2 Mark the predicted height of low water along the bottom line.
3 Join the two marks with a straight line.
4 Write in time of low water and mark in hourly intervals until time required.
5 Draw line from required time vertically to where it touches the curve.
6 Draw horizontal line from the point where the vertical line touches the curve to the diagonal line drawn on left hand side.
7 Read off vertically to find height in metres. In this example 2.3 metres.
So height of tide at Bembridge at 1700 is 2.3 metres.
   This method can be used where there is a curve for the port. If you

are using a secondary port sometimes the curve may be very different from that of the standard port especially if it is not a port on the open coast.

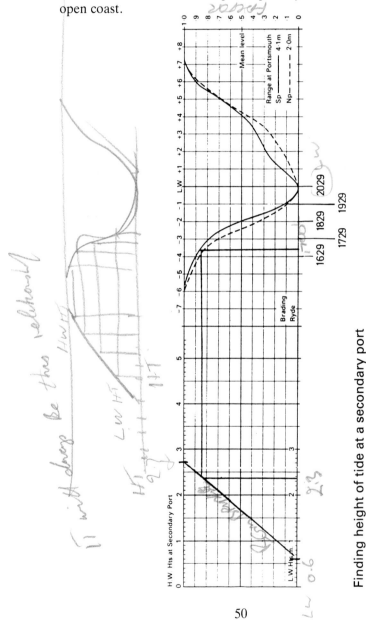

Finding height of tide at a secondary port

Questions

1 Which has the greater range, spring or neap tides?
2 What is the twelfths rule?
3 What is the meaning of semi-diurnal?
4 What are soundings?
5 What do the letters LAT mean?

Exercises

1 Using the tide tables reproduced in this chapter find the time and heights of high water at Dover on June 17
2 Find the times and heights of low water Dover on August 18
3 Find the times and heights of high and low water at Hastings on August 18
4 Find the times and heights of high and low water at Richborough on July 4
5 Using the twelfths rule find the height of the tide at Dover at 0800 BST on August 4
6 Using the tidal curve reproduced in this chapter find the height of the tide at Portsmouth at 1200 BST (use spring curve)
7 Find the height of the tide at Bembridge at 1800 BST on July 2
8 Could a yacht drawing 2 metres enter Bembridge harbour at 1000 BST on May 17?

6

TIDAL STREAMS

Diamonds

Tidal streams are the horizontal movement of water caused by the oscillation of the tides. The rate and direction of this stream obviously influences the course and progress of a small vessel and must be allowed for. Around the British Isles, though not in all waters of the world, the tidal stream is related to the tidal range at the nearest standard port, so that when the range is greatest the tidal stream will be fastest – in other words there is a strong stream at springs and a weaker one at neaps. The navigator needs to know not only the rate but the direction in which the stream is flowing and this is available from a number of sources.

Admiralty Tidal Atlases

These are slim booklets which show hour by hour the change in tidal flow for the area covered. There is a complete page for each hour before and after high water. Often the standard port used as a reference is Dover, which is commonly used as a basis for tidal information affecting the whole of the British Isles. However the Admiralty publish a dozen tidal atlases of home waters and some of these use other convenient standard ports as a basis.

To use a tidal stream atlas on passage first look up the time of high water at the standard port. For example if HW Dover is 1200 and you are leaving your harbour at 0800, you mark 0800 on the page headed '4 Hours Before HW', 0900 on the page called '3 hours before HW' and so on. In this way you have a regular check on the tidal stream, for the duration of your passage, or at least the next 12 hours.

The direction of the tidal streams is shown by black arrows, the heavier and longer ones showing a stronger tidal stream and the smaller, lighter coloured arrows the weaker tidal streams. The figures represent the rate of the tidal stream, the first figure giving the rate at neaps and the second figure giving the rate at springs. The comma indicates the position where the observations were made. For example 12.24 means, 1.2 knots at neaps, 2.4 knots at springs.

12,24

spray

eahs

1.2 knots at neaps

2.4 knots at springs

04,08

neaps springs

0.4 knots at neaps

0.8 knots at springs

Having seen what the stream is doing hour by hour the navigator can then use this information when plotting his EP. Tidal atlases are the quickest and simplest references for this information. A weakness is that the scale is small and so the **set** (the direction in which the stream is flowing) cannot be transferred to the chart with total accuracy. For the same reason tidal atlases cannot show the details of tidal streams setting into bays and inlets. This needs to be watched when sailing a headland to headland course as the tidal set into bays can be considerable and has led to many disasters in the past. Tidal atlases don't go out of date and can be used year after year as long as you have current tide tables to use them with.

Tidal Stream Information On Charts

On every Admiralty chart will be found at intervals a capital letter enclosed by a diamond printed in magenta. To one side of the chart is a table which shows for each of the letters the rate and set of the tide for each hour, with reference to a named standard port. The direction of flow is given as a compass direction. Thus if you find the nearest diamond to your position is E, look for E in the table and check how many hours before or after high water it is at the standard port. If it is two hours before HW then just read off the direction of the tide and its rate on that line under E. Remember to work in GMT. This is likely to be a little more accurate than using a tidal atlas, but does not give you the instant visual impression of the changing pattern over the next few hours that you get from a tidal stream atlas.

Other Sources

Most nautical almanacs contain tidal stream charts similar to the ones in the tidal atlases, but generally on a much smaller scale. These are a useful stand-by if no atlas for the area is to hand. Pilot books and sailing directions contain information on tidal streams where these may need particular attention or caution and should be studied in advance.

Rips, Races and Overfalls

These are different forms of water turbulence which can be dangerous to small vessels. **A race** is caused by a headland protruding into the sea in the path of a fast moving tidal stream – Portland Bill on the Dorset coast is a particularly striking example, but many big headlands have them. They are marked on the charts, but the exact extent of the disturbance and its degree of ferocity changes with the state of the tide. They are of course greater at springs than at neaps. An **overfall** or **rip** is caused by a strong stream near the bottom of the sea being deflected upwards due to an obstruction on the bottom such as a wall of rocks or a sharp change of contour.

The turbulence in these areas is increased by weather conditions, particularly when there is wind over tide and breakers develop which can be seen from some distance. The extent of the disturbance may be as much as two or three miles offshore and it would be prudent to set a course five miles offshore for safe clearance. Often there is a narrow calm channel close inshore at certain states of the tide, but it is as well not to attempt these without local knowledge.

Observation by Buoys, etc

When navigating in confined and busy waters it is just as important to know the strength and direction of the tide and in these circumstances there is not the time as a rule to work out the information as on an open water passage. The skipper must learn to work by

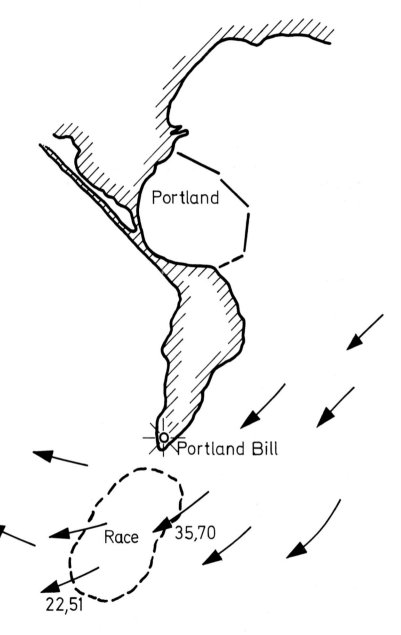

observation. The way boats are laying at their moorings will give one good indication. If the wind is not very strong they are more likely to be tide rode than wind rode. A strong tide will have them straining back on the mooring line, a slack one gently nosing their buoy. Buoys and beacons will lean to the tide and there will be a noticeable rip of water on the down tide side if the flow is strong. Give them a wide berth when passing as the tide can quickly set you down on them.

Questions

1 What publications will show what the tidal stream is doing?
2 Describe an overfall.
3 Where do tidal streams run most strongly?

7
BUOYAGE

Buoys are seamarks to assist safe navigation. They may mark areas of danger or indicate where the safest passage is. They also afford the navigator a check on his position, though this is not their prime function. Buoys are positioned in most cases for the needs of shipping, or at least the biggest vessels likely to be using the area and a yacht may very well find deep water well to the 'wrong' side of a buoy, but it is foolish to take risks unless you know the place well. This is especially the case in shallow waters like the North Sea where deep channels are marked by buoys a long way from land. It is wise to keep to the channels.

IALA System

Buoyage in Northern Europe is now of a uniform type called the IALA (International Association of Lighthouse Authorities) System 'A'. Different systems still operate in other parts of the world. There are five different classifications of buoys whose purposes need to be understood.

Lateral marks used to define a channel
Cardinal marks showing where danger areas exist
Isolated danger marks
Safe water marks
Special marks.

See the colour plates in conjunction with the following sections. Though the word buoy is used throughout here the mark could sometimes be a beacon, pillar or spar with the same characteristics.

Lateral Buoys

These mark the port and starboard sides of deep water navigation channels and are generally found entering harbours and estuaries, though sometimes in open sea if there is a definite channel which needs to be followed.

Port hand buoys are red and can shaped. Some have a red can shaped topmark. At night they might have a red light.
Starboard hand buoys are green and conical shaped. They may have a cone shaped topmark. At night they might have a green light.
The port and starboard hand marking refers to your view when following the channel in from seaward. When leaving a channel it is important to remember to pass the buoys the other way about – leaving green conical buoys to port and red can buoys to starboard. It is a little more difficult when you encounter lateral marks off the coast where it is less obvious which the direction of the channel is. In these cases the buoys are laid according to a conventional direction decided by the authorities. Round the British Isles this conventional direction assumes a 'flow' up the Irish Sea from south to north, up the English Channel from west to east and northwards from the Straits of Dover. If you encounter a lateral buoy away from an obvious entrance channel check on the conventional direction to make sure which side you should leave the buoys. The direction should be marked on the chart with a big open arrow with two dots beside.

Except when using local knowledge it is wise for yachtsmen to follow buoyed channels. However in busy commercial waters yachts can usefully sail close to lateral buoys on the wrong side (i.e. just outside the marked channel). Here they will still have plenty of water beneath the keel, but be out of the way of large working vessels.

Cardinal Marks

These buoys mark shoals or dangers and indicate where the mariner will find navigable water. They are called cardinal marks because they mark the four cardinal points of the compass in relation to the danger. In fact they mark the quadrants from north west to north east, north east to south east, south east to south west and south west to north west. Thus the north end of a group of rocks is marked by a north cardinal buoy and the mariner must pass north of that buoy to clear the rocks. Each of the four cardinal buoys has its own topmark, light and different combination of black and yellow marking. The topmarks are most distinctive with the cardinal buoys and can be seen from some distance. They may be either pillar or spar shaped.

Isolated Danger Mark

This buoy will be placed over a danger which is isolated, but which has navigable water all round it. An example might be a wreck which has sunk in deep water, but with the mast just submerged. The shape is the same as the cardinal buoys (pillar or spar) but the colours are black and red, and the topmarks are two black spheres above each other.

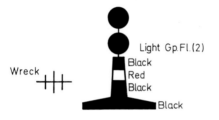

Safe water marks

Used to mark the centre of a wide channel or as landfall buoys. They denote safe water all round.

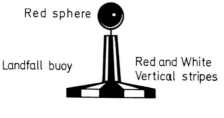

59

Special Marks

All coloured yellow with sometimes a yellow diagonal cross top-mark. A yellow light at night in some cases. These buoys are not for navigation. They may mark cables or pipelines, military exercise areas, spoil grounds, recreation zones or some temporary hazard.

Fish farms

Limitations of Buoys

Although buoys are aids to navigation in the sense that they tell us where it is safe and not safe to go they must be treated with reservation from a position fixing point of view. Many buoys have names clearly painted on their sides and marked on the chart. Sailing near enough to one of these to identify it positively does establish your position. The time of passing should always be noted in the log and the DR position checked against this new information. The sighting of one cannot be relied on however as they are sometimes removed from station temporarily for maintenance or may have dragged off station in prolonged heavy weather. These events are rare but the possibility must be kept in mind. Buoys too far away to be identified are likewise unreliable objects for bearings. They are also not a reliable indication of position at night, even when lit, the light is not a distinguishing one, so there is no certainty which buoy is being seen.

Questions

1 What is a lateral mark?
2 Describe a north cardinal buoy.
3 Which side would it be safe to pass it?
4 Can you use a buoy safely for navigational purposes?
5 You are leaving an estuary and heading to sea when you observe a red cone shaped buoy ahead. Which side should you leave it?

8

LIGHTS

Dangerous points on the coast have been lit for the benefit of mariners for centuries, often by hermits or monks and since the end of the 17th century when the first Eddystone lighthouse was built there have been lights on isolated rocks. To shipping equipped with sophisticated electronic navigation they may no longer be quite as essential as they were, but to the small boat sailor making night passages they are still vital. Many lighthouses now function by remote control and are no longer manned, but this has not diminished their usefulness. Where it was not possible to build a lighthouse to mark a danger lightships were usually employed, moored near shifting sandbanks like the Goodwins. These are now gradually being replaced by Lanbys (standing for Large Automatic Navigational Buoys) which are about 35 feet wide. Though unmanned they have distinguishing lights and cannot be mistaken for ordinary buoys.

Using Lights For Navigation

Lighthouses can be used in a number of ways to assist navigation. By day they are usually architecturally distinctive and easy to identify without doubt. They are also a fixed and unmistakable object affording an accurate bearing. Often the towers are painted in a striking way (say with red and white bands) to making sighting easier. Lightvessels and lanbys have names on their sides in large letters.

By night all lights, whether houses, vessels, beacons or lanbys have their own pattern of light, different to any others in the region, in order that there should be no mistake in identification. This uniqueness is known as the **light characteristic** and is dealt with in

61

detail below. Some lighthouses are also a source of signals for radio direction finding and of sound signals in fog.

The position of lighthouses is marked on Admiralty charts with a star and a flash of magenta colour. The centre of the star denotes the precise position from which you should lay off any bearing on the chart. Lightships are marked with a small boat shape in place of the star and a tiny circle beneath indicates the precise position.

Information on charts

Admiralty charts give the following essential information about lights

Characteristic
Range
Colour
Height
Sound signals
Radio signals

Characteristic

The following are the main types of light with the abbreviations used on the chart. Where there are letters in square brackets after the abbreviations these are new internationally agreed abbreviations which are gradually replacing the older ones.

F	*Fixed.* A constant light
Fl	*Flashing.* A steady, uninterrupted flash.
Gp Fl(2)	*Group Flashing.* Always given with a number which
[Fl(2)]	indicates the number of flashes per group and how often. Thus Gp Fl(3) ev. 10 sec. means flashing in groups of three every 10 seconds.
Qk Fl	*Quick flashing.* Continuously repeated quick flashes
[Q] Qk Fl(2)	*Group quick flashing.* Number of flashes per group and

[Q(2)1]	frequency always shown (e.g. Qk Fl(2) ev 5 sec)
Occ	*Occulting.* A steady light interrupted by a regular short
[Qc]	period of darkness
Gp. Occ(2)	*Group occulting.* Two or more short periods of darkness
[Oc (2)]	in groups. Number and timing shown as for flashing.
Iso.	*Isophase.* Equal periods of light and dark.
Alt. WR	*Alternating.* Showing one colour then another, in this
[A1.WR]	example white and red.
Mo.	*Morse.* A light which represents a letter of the morse alphabet, the letters always being shown in brackets on the chart.

The above list is not exhaustive. The Admiralty record 16 different types of light characteristic, not counting variations of colour, but some of them are only rarely encountered. Lighthouse authorities such as Trinity House take care not to use similar characteristics in the same vicinity. Nevertheless it is quite easy (particularly in the relief of seeing a light after a long passage) to assume it is the one you were expecting to see. It should always be checked by careful timing. A stopwatch is useful, or at least a watch with a good second hand.

Coloured and Sectored Lights

Unless stated to the contrary lights are always white. Red and green are sometimes used, more often on small light beacons marking harbour entrances. Some white lights have a second, coloured light to draw attention to an area of dangerous water. Portland Bill, for instance is Gp.Fl(4) 20 sec., but also displays FR (fixed red) over the Shambles shoals.

Also of importance are sectored lights, where the colour of the main light changes as you move out of the area of safe navigation. A good example is the Needles light at the western approach to the Solent. This is Gp.Occ(2) 20 sec. but the colour of the light changes from white to red over the Shingles Bank and to green as you near the Isle of Wight shore where there are offshore rocks. The chart shows the bearing at which the change takes place from one sector to another.

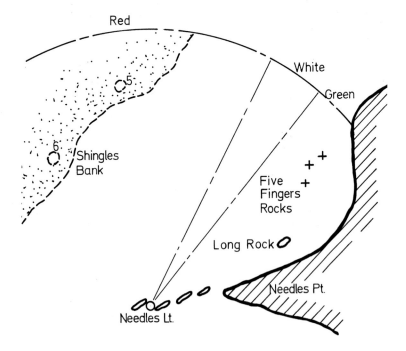

LATERAL BUOYAGE

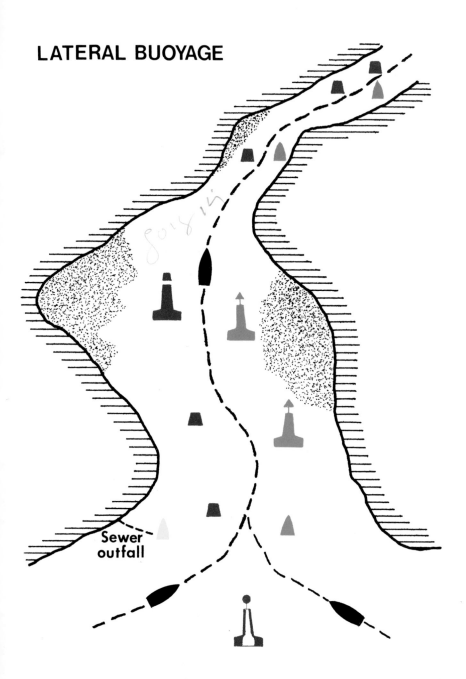

Sewer
outfall

CARDINAL MARKS

PILLAR SHAPED

AREA
OF
DANGER

SPAR SHAPED

North South East West

International Code Flags and Meanings

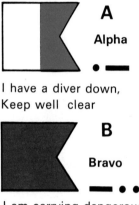

A
Alpha

I have a diver down,
Keep well clear

B
Bravo

I am carrying dangerous
goods

C
Charlie

Yes Affirmative

D
Delta

Keep clear of me - I am
manoeuvring with difficulty

E
Echo

I am altering course to
starboard

F
Foxtrot

I am disabled. Communicate
with me

G
Golf

I require a pilot. Or if fishing,
'I am hauling nets'

H
Hotel

I have a pilot on board

I
India

I am altering course to port

J
Juliett

I am on fire and have a dangerous
cargo on board, keep clear of me

K

Kilo

▬ ● ▬

I wish to communicate with you

P

Papa

● ▬ ▬ ●

All persons should report on board as the vessel is about to sail

L

Lima

● ▬ ● ●

You should stop your vessel instantly

Q

Quebec

▬ ▬ ● ▬

My vessel is healthy and I request free pratique

M

Mike

▬ ▬

My vessel is stopped and making no way through the water

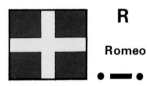

R

Romeo

● ▬ ●

No meaning assigned to this letter

N

November

▬ ●

No, negative

S

Sierra

● ● ●

I am operating astern propulsion

O

Oscar

▬ ▬ ▬

Man overboard

T

Tango

▬

Keep well clear of me, I am engaged in pair trawling

U
Uniform
●● ▬

You are running into danger

X
Xray
▬ ●● ▬

Stop carrying out your intentions and watch for my signals

V
Victor
●●● ▬

I require assistance

Y
Yankee
▬ ● ▬ ▬

I am dragging my anchor

W
Whisky
● ▬ ▬

I require medical assistance

Z
Zulu
▬ ▬ ●●

I require a tug. When made by fishing vessels 'I am shooting nets'

Code and answering pendant

Note. Not all the single letter signals may be made by Morse as an alternative to the flags. Letters B, C, D, E, G, H, I, M, S, T & Z have meanings in the Collision Regulations and should only be made by sound in that context.

VESSEL	LIGHTS/ASPECT				SOUND SIGNAL IN FOG	SHAPE (IF ANY)
	AHEAD	ASTERN	PORT	ST'B'D		
POWER DRIVEN						—
POWER DRIVEN (less than 12m)					an efficient sound signal	—
POWER DRIVEN TOWING						200 m +
BEING TOWED						200 m +
SAILING						

VESSEL	LIGHTS/ASPECT				SOUND SIGNAL IN FOG	SHAPE (IF ANY)
	AHEAD	ASTERN	PORT	ST'B'D		
PILOT VESSEL					and	
VESSEL AT ANCHOR					Bell & gong if 100 m+	
VESSEL CONSTRAINED BY DRAFT						
VESSEL AGROUND					Bell & Gong	
POWER DRIVEN (less than 7 m)					an efficient sound signal	

VESSEL	LIGHTS/ASPECT				SOUND SIGNAL IN FOG	SHAPE (IF ANY)
	AHEAD	ASTERN	PORT	ST'B'D		
FISHING						
TRAWLING						
NOT UNDER COMMAND						
RESTRICTED MANOEUVRABILITY						

Range of Light

The distance from which a light can be seen is obviously important to the navigator, but it can be expressed in three different ways. **Luminous range** is the distance depending only on the intensity of the light source and the prevailing meteorological conditions. **Nominal range** is what the luminous range would be if visibility at the time was 10 miles **Geographical range** is the maximum distance a light could be seen in perfect conditions, allowing for curvature of the earth, the height of the light and the height of the observer.

The Admiralty have at various times used all three of these ranges as the one marked on the chart, but charts made during the last 15 years have used nominal range. The geographical range is the one of most interest to yachtsmen as it enables a position to be found from the rising and dipping distances.

Bearing of lights

Charts will often show bearings with lights to define the arc through which the light can be seen. All these bearings are given from seaward to the light and they are always true bearings (not magnetic). At night they afford a useful position line if you can note the moment of a light becoming visible or disappearing as you cross the track of the beam.

Height of Light

Knowing the height of the light is useful for navigation when using rising and dipping lights and also for finding position with a vertical sextant angle. Heights are given on the chart in metres. This is a height above MHWS not the height of the building itself which can be a very different thing. For instance Berry Head lighthouse in Devon claims to be both the tallest and smallest in England. The automatic tower is only a few feet high, but it stands on a massive clifftop, so the charted height is 58 metres. Because heights are above MHWS allowance should be made for the tide in all calculations if the light has a very low elevation above sea level. In other cases this is not necessary for practical purposes.

Sound Signals

Not all lights have fog signalling apparatus. The information is marked on the chart where they do, using the following notations.

Dia	*Diaphone*. Powerful low pitched sound ending with a noticeable grunt. Works on compressed air.
Horn	*Horn*. Can be electric or compressed air. A very powerful sound which can be a steady note or varying in pitch.
Siren	*Siren*. Compressed air apparatus. Sound differs with type
Reed	*Reed*. High pitched sound. Can be rather weak.
Explos.	*Explosive signal*, like a gun going off.

Fog signals cannot be relied on for navigation for reasons discussed in the chapter on sailing in bad visibility. Some buoys are also fitted with sound signals, bells or whistles activated automatically. There are also bell buoys activated by wave motion which sound all the time.

Radio Facilities

Some lighthouses are fitted with radio beacons making continuous transmissions of a signal which can be used to obtain bearings with a radio direction finding set. These are marked RoBn on the chart. Each transmits a distinguishing group of two or three letters of the Morse code – Portland Bill is PB, Eddystone is DY, etc. These are listed in nautical almanacs and arranged in groups which afford convenient cross bearings.

Some lighthouses are fitted with Racon (marked RC on chart). This is a radar responder which gives off a signal when triggered by the vessel's radar set.

Information About Lights

There are more detailed sources of information about lights than that shown on the chart and there are sometimes reasons why these should be consulted. Smaller lights, particularly those marking harbour entrances and channels, may not appear on a particular chart because the scale is too small to show them. Or you may want to be sure of the geographical range. The definitive source of information is the Admiralty List of Lights, published in 12 volumes covering the world. The first covers the British Isles and adjacent coasts. New editions are published every 18 months and they can be kept up to date in between from the weekly Notices to Mariners. Principal lighthouses, which are those with a geographical range of over 15 miles, are listed in bold type and lesser lights in ordinary type. Lightships are shown in italic. The details given are much more comprehensive than on the chart and specify the type of range, together with tables for making use of this information in calculating distance off, etc.

The principal nautical almanacs also give much of this information. Reed's lists lights for every part of the British Isles and many stretches of Continental coast. The listing includes not just navigational lights but all those marking harbour entrances and lit buoys in channels leading up many small anchorages. The Macmillan Silk Cut Yachtsman's Almanac has a similar list of lights.

Questions

1 List the information usually found on charts about a lighthouse.
2 What is an occulting light?
3 Where can you find information about lighthouses in addition to the charts?
4 The chart shows Bass Rock light in Scotland as GpF1(6) 30 sec. Describe what you would see.
5 What is the geographical range of a light?

9

PILOTAGE

This section of the syllabus is concerned with the safe conduct of yachts in and out of harbours. Before approaching any strange harbour a skipper must make himself as knowledgeable as possible about it, from the chart, nautical almanacs and pilot books. Nearly all ports have professional pilots, registered by Trinity House, whose job is to conduct ships in and out of port. For large ships the employment of a pilot is compulsory in some places, though never for yachts. If you ever did want one (the fees might be high) his services could be summoned by VHF or by making (by flag or light) the Morse letter G.

Harbour Regulations and Control Signals

Harbourmasters have considerable legal powers over the movement of vessels within their jurisdiction. There may be all kinds of local regulations which they can enforce concerning speed, entry, moorings, etc. In some circumstances they may even stop a vessel leaving. It is always prudent to ask at the Harbourmaster's Office about any points on which you are unsure and always wise to heed the Harbourmaster's advice. Nautical almanacs will list the lights, buoys and beacons which mark a harbour. In the absence of a very large scale chart study carefully the harbour plans published in one of the various yachting pilot books for popular cruising areas to see where the deep water channels are, how they are marked and where suitables moorings or anchorage may be had. They should also give important local regulations. Portsmouth, for example, prohibits yachts which have auxiliary engines from proceeding under sail within the confines of the harbour, while the use of spinnakers is prohibited on the River Hamble north of Warsash jetty.

Port Control Signals

In busy ports you are likely to encounter port entry signals which control when vessels may enter and not. These are listed in the nautical almanac (alphabetically in Reed's, unlike lights and buoys which are listed in coastwise order). For example: At Dover (an exceptionally busy place) three red lights vertically at night or three red balls by day, forbid any vessels to enter, including yachts. At Honfleur in France the international code flag P, or at night three white lights, shows that the lock gates to the basin are open. At Weymouth two green flags or two green lights forbid you to leave because a vessel is approaching the harbour mouth from seaward. There is no common national or international system with regard to port control signals. A skipper must look up the information in advance and make a note of it for instant reference.

Planning

The importance of planning in advance all pilotage operations cannot be stressed too much. A close study of all information to be gleaned from charts, almanacs and pilot books should provide a clear mental picture of harbours and anchorages to be entered. You should know in advance the names of buoys, the shape of the navigable channel, the likely anchorages or berths, leading marks and the whereabouts of any dangers like rocks or shoals. You should also have listed the courses to steer between marks in case of bad visibility. This should be studied in detail for all harbours it is intended to visit and it is prudent to have assimilated the main features of any others in the intended sailing area to which you might have to go because of adverse weather conditions, or any other cause which results in a change of plan.

Leading Marks

Well worth noting in advance are leading marks which offer a safe line of approach into an anchorage, especially as these are often found in small places with few other navigational markings. Leading marks are any two objects which, when kept in line, provide a bearing along which it is safe to steer. These are usually mentioned in pilot books and sometimes marked on charts. Two beacons, one behind the other, are a common form of leading mark. Or one beacon on a rock may be combined with a prominent object on the shore. Two large rocks painted white do duty as leading marks in some Scottish lochs. The marks may not be easy to distinguish from seaward and may have to be picked out with binoculars as you approach. In steering on them allowance must be made for leeway and current pushing the yacht off the bearing.

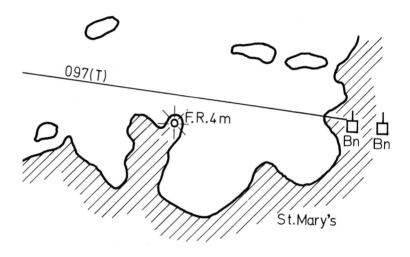

Clearing Lines

These are an excellent dodge for piloting safely into a strange harbour which does not have a buoyed channel. Sometimes they are marked on charts, but more often you will have to find your own. Taking any prominent object ashore draw a line along one side of the approach, extended seawards and clear of all dangers and shallow water. Read off and note the bearing. Do the same on the other side. In the example illustrated you would then have two bearings of 005 and 345. You can therefore safely approach on any course which is between these two figures. If you are tacking it is safe to make boards which do not take you beyond a point where a bearing from the yacht to the object ashore would be outside these figures.

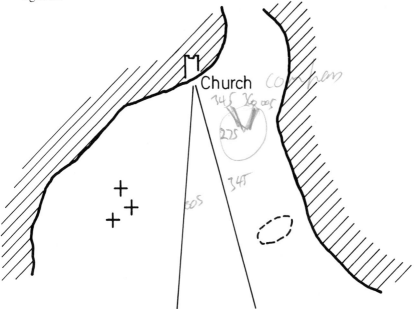

Church

Reminders

Don't cut corners round points of land or shoal banks
Keep to the starboard side of channels
Never try to pass ahead of other craft in the channel
Remember that deepest water is always on the outside of bends
Give way to large craft which need the deep water
Pass buoys and moored craft with good clearance in case the tide sets you down on them
Have your anchor ready to let go. If sailing engine ready to use, if motoring sails ready to hoist for emergency
Call for local guidance on VHF if necessary.

Questions

1 What are clearing lines?
2 What is the purpose of a leading mark?
3 What precautions would you take when navigating in a harbour?

10
ECHO SOUNDERS

At any time approaching an anchorage or strange stretch of coast-line, or whenever there may be the least doubt about there being sufficient water ahead to avoid risk of going around, a skipper must be able to check the depth of water. The majority of craft to-day are fitted with echo sounders. Like other delicate equipment at sea they are capable of 'going on the bleep' and an acquaintance with older depth finding methods is desirable.

Echo Sounder Types

Two main types are found in yachts. Both work by sending a supersonic signal to the seabed and timing the echo which the instrument then converts into a depth measurement.

Rotating dial echo sounder.

Rotating dial. In this type a rotating dial gives an electronic or neon flash indicating the depth. It generally has two scales, one for deep and the other for shallow water operation and has to be set on the right scale by the operator. The depth flash is clear but with this type the figures on the scale can be difficult to distinguish clearly in strong sunlight and at night. Having two scales can give rise to a 'second trace' which can be misleading. If for instance you are working on the shallow water scale and this reads up to a maximum of 25 metres depth and you were actually sailing in water giving a 30 metre echo the dial would do a complete circuit and show a depth of 5 metres. If in doubt about whether you are suddenly in unexpected shallow water switch over to the deep scale to compare readings.

Pointer Type. This works on only one depth scale and a finger on a dial points to the depth. More up to date models with a digital readout are also available. This type is generally less sophisticated, but clearer and simpler to use.

Modern pointer type echo sounder with digital reading

Cautions in use

Echo sounders are capable of false echoes, a shoal of fish being the commonest cause. The second trace effect on the rotating dial type also has to be watched for. Many models are capable of operating in either feet and fathoms or metres at the turn of a switch and it is important to be aware which you are operating in. If you have a choice you should switch to match the soundings of the chart you are currently using. The echoes which measure the depth are sent from a device called a transducer which is attached to the outside of the hull at any point below the waterline. It is important to remember that the depth measured will be from the transducer. Skippers should know the distance between the transducer and the bottom of the keel and make allowance for this. It is possible to have some models of echo sounder professionally calibrated to give a reading corrected for keel depth. Some are also fitted with an alarm which can be set to a pre-determined depth.

The Lead Line

Before the days of echo sounders depth was found by 'heaving the lead', a lead weight around 10 lb on the end of a line which might be 25 fathoms (150 feet) or more in length. Small craft would have a 7 lb lead and less line, but the lines were always marked in the same way – 2 strips of leather at 2 fathoms, white calico at 5 fathoms, leather with a hole at 10 and many more. This was not just tradition but a way of ensuring that any able bodied seaman could find himself aboard any ship and know just what he was doing, even in the dark in a gale. An experienced leadsman could sing out a depth to within a quarter of a fathom (18 inches!) with the ship moving at 10 knots.

There is no compelling reason why a yachtsman should use the traditional markings, but handiness with a lead is useful. Any suitable weight and a set of home-made markings would do. If the vessel is stopped it is a simple matter to drop the 'lead' over the side and check the depth of water (which in this case will be from the waterline, not under the keel). Under way the operation needs a little more practice. The line must be gathered in coils (like a heaving line) and, after swinging to gain momentum, heaved ahead. The leadsman gathers in the slack as the vessel moves forward so that he can note the marks as the line comes taut up and down with the lead on the bottom.

Questions

1 What is the transducer?
2 When would you use your echo sounder?
3 Is there any value in carrying a lead line?

11

RADIO AIDS TO NAVIGATION

The use of radio and electronic navigation systems for small boats is developing rapidly. The modern yachtsman must be competent in their use. The chief danger is to place total reliance on them. Opportunities for visual position fixing should be used at intervals.

Radio Direction Finding

Radio beacons are sited around coasts and on some isolated rock stations, often though not always in association with lighthouses. The signals they transmit can be used to obtain a bearing with a special radio receiver which has a direction finding aerial (an RDF set) and incorporates a compass. There are a dozen such stations on the English side of the Channel and even more on the French side. About each one the navigator needs the following information which can be found in the Admiralty List of Radio Stations, or in any of the regular nautical almanacs:

Its location so it can be found on the chart
The transmission frequency
Its range
Identifying signal
Pattern of transmission

This information cannot be found from the chart, though the stations are marked with a magenta circle and the letters RoBn. The identifying signal is a group of two morse letters which is transmitted at intervals for about a minute. As with visual fixes a bearing will provide only a position line, but the stations are arranged in groups all transmitting on the same frequency so that there is always an opportunity to take a series of cross bearings. To facilitate this the stations in the group, which will generally number between four and six, transmit in turn. The order of transmission is listed with the other information so that navigators know which one to try and tune to next. The range of these signals may be anything from 10 to 50 miles.

Radio bearings are subject to some errors and should be checked with visual bearings when opportunity offers.

Night Effect Radio bearings become unreliable during the period one hour before sunset to one hour after sunrise. The effect is more noticeable at distances over 20 miles from the beacon and at more than 50 miles from the beacon become very unreliable.

Coastal Refraction If the radio bearing being used is at 90 degrees to the coast then there is no effect, but if the wave is crossing the coast at a shallow angle the radio wave is bent in towards the land. As this will give a fix closer to the coast than you really are it is an error on the safe side.

A is the bearing the vessel would receive
B is the bearing the vessel should receive without coastal refraction
C is the bearing at right angles to the coast when there is no error.

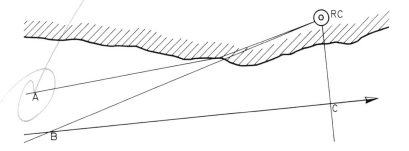

Half Convergency This an error due to the fact that radio waves follow a curve or great circle and not a straight line. They are only of concern over very long distances and there are tables in the nautical almanacs explaining the correction of half convergency.

Quadrantal Error This is caused by radiation from the metal structures or rigging of the vessel and can be corrected by insulation or by fitting rope seizings in place of shackles at strategic points.

Air Beacons

Sometimes these may be more convenient to use than marine radio beacons. They give a better signal, are usually more powerful and transmit continuously.

Radio Direction Finding and Radio Lighthouses

These are marked on the chart with the letters RG. The lighthouse will take a bearing of the vessel and relay that bearing. The vessel has to transmit a series of long dashes while the lighthouse takes the bearing. There are only a few such lighthouses round the British Isles, but include Rame Head, Berry Head, South Foreland and Flamborough Head. These lighthouses also operate a VHF emergency D/F service.

VHF Radio Lighthouse

The lighthouse transmits a series of beats which can be picked up on an ordinary VHF set on Channel 88 (162.025 MHz) by counting the beats identification can be made from tables in the nautical almanacs and a bearing of the lighthouse obtained. To provide a fix the lighthouses have been arranged in pairs. The system is still experimental and may be discontinued or altered without warning, but it does provide an accurate position.

Radar

Radar will give excellent immediate position if you are near enough to a coastline. Operation of the set with knowledge of how to use it is important and there are courses for yachtsmen who wish to improve their skills.

Types of DF receiver

Hand sets with ferrite rod or loop aerials are still the most extensively used in yachts. To obtain the bearing the set is turned until a null (an eclipse or low point in the signal) is reached and the bearing is then read off on the compass. The reason the null is the correct point and not the loudest signal is that the greatest strength is received when the antenna is at right angles to the signal. An occasional danger in this system is that it can give a reading which is the reciprocal of the true bearing, but a 180 degree error should be too obvious to deceive the navigator. Modern sets using this system can lock on to the beacons and give a continuous position and read out.

Hyperbolic and Satellite Systems

Highly sophisticated navigation systems using micro computers are fast coming within the range of the average yacht owner. Hyperbolic systems like Decca, Loran and Consol interpret transmissions from earth stations and translate them into a latitude and longitude position. They have ranges of hundreds of miles and in the right conditions can have an almost pinpoint accuracy. At the extent of their range and at night they are subject to more error.

Satellite systems pick up signals from orbiting satellites and on board computers use this to determine the position. Some of this equipment such as SatNav is extremely compact and simple to use. It is very accurate and almost its only potential weakness is battery failure which should be watched out for.

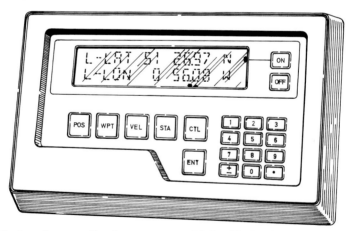

Modern log reading instrument which will give both speed and distance run

Waypoints

These are positions given in latitude and longitude of key navigation points (lights, buoys, etc) around the coast and listed in nautical almanacs, enabling the navigator to readily work out the courses and distances from one to the other. Some of the modern electronic navigation systems are capable of providing instant information about these, while at the same time doing all the necessary calculations about tidal streams, leeway correction and estimated times of arrival.

Questions

1 How do you obtain a radio bearing?
2 How are radio beacons marked on a chart?
3 What is a waypoint?
4 What can a Decca system give you?
5 Are radio bearings completely reliable?

12
SPEED AND DISTANCE MEASURING

[handwritten margin note: r knot be hr = 5 naut. mile per hr]

Knowing the ship's speed and the distance it has travelled is an essential ingredient in navigation. Some of the electronic systems discussed in the last chapter incorporate this function but a knowledge of other methods is needed. An instrument for measuring speed and distance is called a **log**. Speed is measured in **knots** (nautical miles per hour).

[handwritten margin notes: Set distance log (hr) → speed. Can check log (distance) by say t hr × hr to get distance. then look of the log (distance) should Be the same.]

The Towed Log

The most common type of log until quite recently was one which towed a rotator astern on a line. The line is attached to a dial mounted inboard on the transom or counter and this shows the distance travelled. The best known of this type is the Walker's Patent Log of which many thousands are still in use, but there are other makes and the more modern ones show speed as well as distance. It is important to realise that these logs record the distance travelled through the water, not the distance made good over the ground. They are very reliable and mainly accurate, though liable to under-record in light airs when there is not much way on. The log is usually streamed when the departure position is plotted after leaving harbour so that it can be used from there to maintain a DR plot.

A snag about this kind of log is that it can become fouled with weed and it has been known for the rotator to be taken by sharks. And if you forget to take it in after making your landfall the line may foul your own or somebody else's propeller as you enter harbour. Also if you don't remember to 'end for end' the line over the stern to 'unwind' it before taking it in you end up with a mammoth tangle.

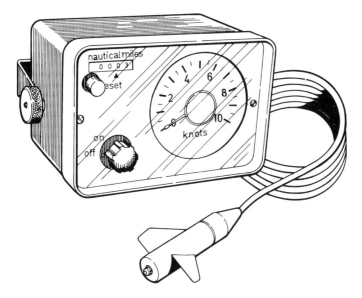

Impeller Logs

Modern satellite navigation sets for yachts give a read out of exact position by latitude and longitude.

81

These are electromagnetic logs with an impeller which rotates and sends impulses to an instrument through a transducer. They have to be fitted through the hull but the display can be located anywhere convenient for the navigator. They generally operate from their own batteries. Speed and distance are displayed continuously whenever the log is switched on. Impeller logs also register only speed and distance through the water, so allowances for tidal stream have to be made. The transducers can become foul and should be inspected whenever the vessel is slipped or dried out.

Doppler Logs give distance made good.

These make ultrasonic measurements from inside the hull and are the only type which give speed and distance over the ground as opposed to through the water and can therefore be a great advantage in tidal conditions. They need to be calibrated very accurately or they may over-read by as much as 15 per cent.

Dutchman's Log

Suppose you had no log, or it was out of action. You are out of sight of land and uncertain about the progress you are making. But at least you know the length of your boat in feet or metres. A chip of wood or a matchbox dropped over the bows and timed as it passes the stern will enable you to work out, by simple arithmetic, how long it will take you to sail a mile (6080 ft or 1,852 metres).

Questions

1 Two types of logs measure distance travelled through the water. Which are they?
2 Which type measures distance over the ground?
3 What are the disadvantages of a towed log?

13

THE LOG BOOK

The log book, also called the deck log, or just simply the log, is the official navigational record of a voyage. It gets its name because it records, among other information, the periodic readings of the distance measuring log. It is not just big ship practice or a tradition. Every efficient yacht skipper will keep a log. There are four reasons for doing so.

1. A log book can be produced as valid evidence in a court of law if you were involved as a party or witness in any action as a result of an incident at sea such as a collision or sinking. It needs to have been signed, witnessed and dated at the time.
2. Your insurers may accept it as proof that you have taken all seamanlike precautions in the event of some claim.
3. It provides a record of all your principal navigation actions during a passage. If you become unsure of your position or have cause to doubt your last plot you may be able to check your chartwork from the information in the log.
4. Though this is not strictly important, the log provides a pleasant permanent reminder of times at sea. A deck log tends to become a bit battered and tea stained, but many people like to make a fair copy at the end of the voyage and decorate it with photographs, sketches, etc.

Information to be recorded

Log books can be purchased from chandlers, printed with appropriate columns. If you don't want to buy one of these a ruled exercise book will do just as well. The following entries should be made regularly

Course being steered
Wind strength and direction
Barometer reading
Distance recorded on log

It is usual to make these entries hourly, though in fairly un-eventful conditions or on a long passage every two hours, or at the change of watch every four hours, would do.

The following entries should be made as they occur, noting the time.

Changes of course (with a log reading)
Times of entering and leaving harbour
Times of passing lighthouses, buoys or other navigation objects
Times of stopping and starting engine

Most logs have a general remarks column in which it is useful to record such information as

Changes to sail being carried
Notable sightings of other vessels
Maintenance needs for future action,
Wildlife observations if they interest you
Sea state
Visibility

The log for each passage should be headed up with the intended destination. In the case of sailing vessels there is a long standing custom that this should be written as Passage *Towards* Roscoff rather than Passage To Roscoff, presumably so as not to tempt the fates. At the start of each cruise it may be useful to record the names of the crew and if you are watchkeeping showing the leader and members of each watch

Questions

1 Can the log be a legal document?
2 List some items you might record in your log.

July 10th — Yarmouth towards Cherbourg

TIME	COURSE	LOG RDG	WIND	BAROMETER	REMARKS
0700	As req.	—	SW 3	1012	Left moorings under engine
0720	230	3	SW4	1012	Stopped engine. Set all plain sail. Needles Lt. Ho. to port.
0730	180	5	SW4	1013	Set genoa.
1000		12	SW2	1013	Drizzle.
1100			SSW2	1014	Started engine
1200	180	22	Lt airs	1014	Motor sailing
1300	175	26	Lt airs	1013	RDF posn St Catherine's bearing 013
1330			SW3		Stopped engine
1400	175	30	SW3	1012	
1600	175	43	SW6	998	Handed genoa, set No.1 jib. One reef in main. Rain. Viz one mile

14

METEOROLOGY

A yachtmaster is required to be familiar with all basic meteorological terms, to have a knowledge of weather systems and cloud types, to be able to understand and interpret weather forecasts and to know what the influence of local conditions will be.

Meteorological Terms

Air Mass a mass of air which has formed over a section of the earth's surface and has developed certain properties which will determine the weather in the region.

Anemometer an instrument which measures the speed of the wind.

Angle of Indraft the angle between an isobar and the actual direction of the wind.

Anticyclone an area of relatively high pressure and little wind. Also known as a **high**.

Backing a change in the wind direction in an anti clockwise direction, for example the wind is backing if it shifts from the SW to SE.

Col an area situated between two high pressure areas and two low pressure areas.

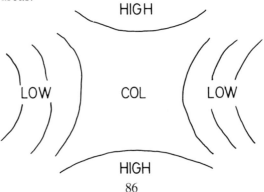

Cyclone a tropical revolving storm.

Depression an area of relatively low pressure associated with strong winds revolving around the centre of the depression. Also known as a **low**.

Dew air which has cooled on contact with a colder surface at night, condensed and formed visible water droplets.

Dew Point the lowest temperature to which air can be cooled without causing condensation.

Doldrums an area near the equator associated with calms and heavy rain.

Front the line which separates a cold air mass from a warm air mass.

Inversion the temperature of air usually decreases with height but occasionally the reverse happens and the rising air becomes warmer.

Isobars lines on a weather map showing places with equal pressure at sea level.

Katabatic wind air which has been cooled and flows down from a mountainous area.

Occlusion when the warm sector of a depression has been lifted off the surface by the cold front behind.

Ridge an extension to an anticyclone which forms a wedge of high pressure.

Squall strong gusting wind usually accompanied by a rapid change in direction.

Trough the opposite of a ridge of high pressure. The trough is the line through the centre of the depression shown by a rising and falling barometer.

Veering a change of wind in a clockwise direction.

Backing

Wind

Wind is the flow of air across the surface of the earth. It is caused by the differing pressure systems around the world which are in turn caused by temperature differences around the surface of the Earth. In comparison to the sea the land heats up very quickly and cools down very quickly thus giving rise to different barometric pressures. The diagram below illustrates the general global picture of winds and pressure systems which is basically correct but is a big generalisation as local conditions will often prevail.

The Trade winds blow continuously from high to low or from about 35 degrees north and south towards the equator. There is at the equator an area known as the Doldrums which persist about 5 degrees either side of the equator where there is little wind and persistent heavy rain. The winds would in fact blow due north and south if it was not for the rotation of the earth which deflects them in the directions shown. The whole wind systems of the world tend to move north and south with the annual movement of the sun. The westerlies in the northern hemisphere tend to be more variable than those in the southern hemisphere due to the greater land mass. This causes the westerly wind in the south to blow more strongly and they are known as the Roaring Forties in latitude 40S.

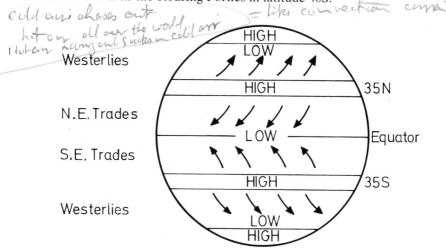

Wind is caused by local heating and cooling and a good example is the occurrence of the monsoons over India and China. The large land mass of Europe and Asia heats up during the summer and causes a large low pressure to occur. As the warm air rises then cooler air moves in to take its place causing the south west monsoon in the northern summer, which can blow very strongly from June to September. The reverse happens in winter when the land cools down more quickly than the sea and so a high pressure develops over the continent with winds flowing outwards from the high pressure area giving the north east monsoon in winter. These winds tend to blow less strongly. A similar effect can be felt on a smaller scale off the coasts of Portugal and Spain where local winds can reach gale force due to the heating of the land mass during the day.

Wind force is measured by the Beaufort Scale used in all the weather forecasts, and all yachtsmen must be familiar with it.

No.	m.p.h.	Name	Conditions
0	Less than 1	Calm	Sea like a mirror
1	1–3	Light air	Ripples with the appearance of scales are formed but without foam crests.
2	4–6	Light breeze	Small wavelets, still short but more pronounced. Crests have a glassy appearance and do not break.
3	7–10	Gentle breeze	Large wavelets. Crests begin to break. Foam of glassy appearance. Perhaps scattered white horses.
4	11–16	Moderate breeze	Small waves, becoming longer: fairly frequent horses.
5	17–21	Fresh breeze	Moderate waves, taking a more pronounced long form; many white horses are formed (chance of some spray).
6	22–27	Strong breeze	Large waves begin to form; the white foam crests are more extensive everywhere (probably some spray).
7	28–33	Near gale	Sea heaps up and white foam from breaking waves begins to be blown in streaks along the direction of the wind.
8	34–40	Gale	Moderately high waves of greater length; edges of crests begin to break into spindrift. The foam is blown in well-marked streaks along the direction of the wind.
9	41–47	Strong gale	High waves. Dense streaks of foam along the direction of the wind. Crests of waves begin to topple, tumble and roll over. Spray may effect visibility.
10	48–55	Storm	Very high waves with long overhanging crests. The resulting foam in great patches is blown in dense white streaks along the direction of the wind. On the whole the surface of the sea takes a white appearance. The tumbling of the sea becomes heavy and shocklike. Visibility affected.
11	56–63	Violent storm	Exceptionally high waves. (Small and medium-sized ships might be for a time lost to view behind the waves). The sea is completely covered with long white patches of foam lying along the direction of the wind. Everywhere the edges of the wave crests are blown into froth. Visibility affected.
12	64+	Hurricane	The air is filled with foam and spray. Sea completely white with driving spray; visibility very seriously affected.

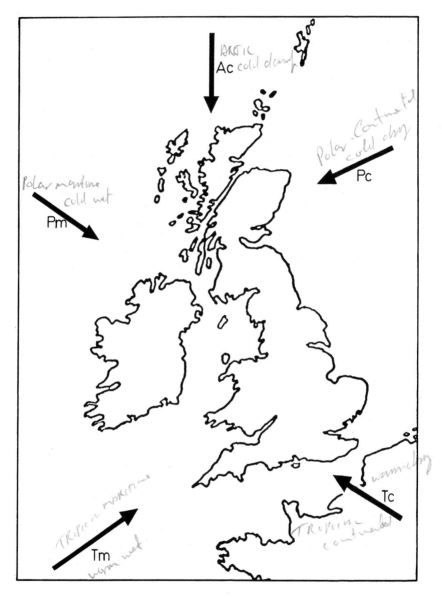

Arctic
Ac cold damp

Polar Continental
cold dry
Pc

Polar maritime
cold wet
Pm

Tropical maritime
warm wet
Tm

warm dry
Tc

Tropical
continental

90

Air Masses

The weather we experience is associated with air masses which originate in distant parts of the world. Some time ago a layer of fine red dust settled on the southern part of England and this originated from the Sahara Desert, which meant that a warm air mass from that area had moved northwards. The diagram shows the main origins of air masses affecting the British Isles. Pm = Polar Maritime. This is air which has originated in cold Arctic regions and has become wet as it crosses the Atlantic. Tm = Tropical Maritime and is air which originates in the tropics, moving north over the Atlantic so it is warm and wet. Tc = Tropical continental which originates from the continent of Europe or Africa, producing a warm dry air mass because it has travelled over land. Pc = Polar continental and comes overland from Siberia, so it is a cold dry air mass. Ac = Arctic and comes directly from the Arctic as very cold and damp air.

These air masses determine the type of weather systems that will develop over the British Isles.

Cloud Types

Recognition of clouds is a very good way of finding out what the local weather is likely to be doing in the next 24 hours. They are signs indicating the prevailing weather patterns and if you can recognise some of the cloud types then you will be able to make your own short term forecast fairly accurately.

Clouds can be divided into four main groups:

High clouds which include cirrus, cirro cumulus and cirro stratus

Middle clouds which include alto-cumulus, alto-stratus and nimbo-stratus

Low clouds which include strato-cumulus and stratus

Low clouds with vertical extent which include cumulus and cumulo-nimbus

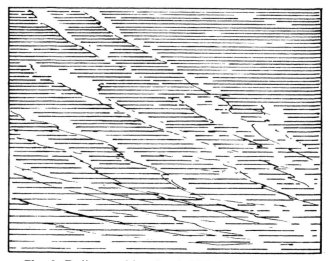

Cirrus Clouds Delicate white clouds high in the sky often in lines and curves. Hooked cirrus (or 'mares tails') indicate an imminent change in the weather.

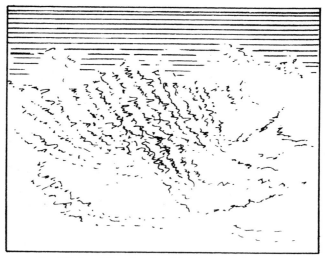

Cirrocumulus High white clouds which have a rippled effect. They are often in lines and can cover a large part of the sky. They usually indicate that unsettled weather is approaching.

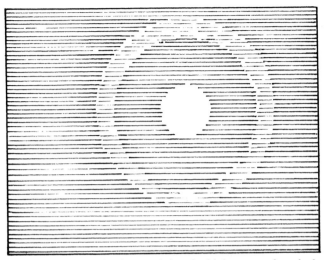

Cirrostratus A thin white layer of cloud which covers the whole sky. It will often give a halo effect and indicates poor weather approaching.

Altocumulus often cover the whole sky to give a cotton wool effect. Usually indicates fair weather but with thundery outbreaks.

middle **Altostratus** A continuous layer of grey cloud over the whole sky. Rain may begin to fall. A middle level cloud sometimes becoming very low.

Low middle **Stratocumulus** Large dark grey rolls of cloud, often very heavy looking, which cover the whole sky at low level. Often obscures headlands and higher ground. It indicates settled weather but with occasional rain.

94

Cumulus White clouds floating in the sky of cauliflower like appearance. They can be fairly high, reaching up vertically into the sky, not covering the whole sky but floating independently. They indicate fair weather.

Cumulonimbus Heavy masses of cloud reaching great heights vertically. Often the top will spread out into an anvil shape. They often herald hailstorms and squalls with a sudden change of wind direction, and possibly thunder and lightning.

Some of the old weather rhymes associated with clouds are worth remembering. Their originators may not have known whether they had any scientific basis, but they were based on observation.

Red sky at night shepherds delight
Red sky in the morning shepherds warning.

An evening red sky will be caused by the setting sun reflecting on middle or higher clouds which often indicate better weather, but a red sky in the morning may be caused by the sun reflecting on lower clouds which will indicate bad weather. But the clouds have to be studied carefully to see if the rhyme makes sense in the context of other factors. Another rhyme says

If clouds are gathering thick and fast
Keep sharp lookout for sail and mast
But if they slowly onward crawl
Shoot your lines, nets and trawl.

This applies to low scudding clouds which are moving quickly round a depression thus indicating bad weather. Slow moving cloud is often a stratus type cloud which does not give too much cause for concern.

High Pressure Systems

An area of high pressure is usually associated with light winds and fine weather. The winds in the northern hemisphere blow clockwise round a high and are usually light. In the summer an area of high pressure will produce long spells of fine weather because high pressure areas are slow moving and can last for a week or so. Visibility may not be very good and there will often be a sea haze. Areas of high pressure will often divert areas of low pressure and cause depressions to move away north or south of the British Isles. In the wintertime a high pressure area will give clear skies and very cold weather, but usually dry. On the weather charts the isobars will be far apart indicating light winds. The diagram shows an area of high pressure over the British Isles. Note that the winds follow the isobars in direction and are blowing clockwise round the high. High

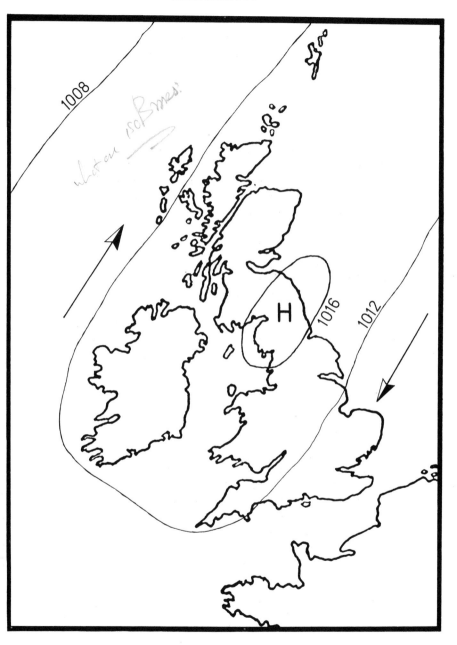

1008

what are isobars?

1016

1012

H

pressure systems are sometimes called **anti cyclones** and we talk about anti cyclonic conditions. **Ridges of high pressure** are mentioned in the shipping forecast and these are really only small areas of high pressure sandwiched between areas of low pressure. They will bring fine weather for a shorter period of time

Low presure systems

circular air production movement year

Low pressure systems are more complex than high pressure systems. Low pressure systems (or **depressions**) usually form out in the Atlantic and move in a north easterly direction at about 20 to 25 knots. The whole system is moving in that direction while the winds are blowing quite strongly anti clockwise (in the northern hemisphere) round its centre. The isobars tend to be close together, depending upon the depth of the low pressure centre. Depressions bring with them wind, rain, mist, cloud and fog. Gales are usually centred around depressions and with a very deep depression storm force winds can occur.

Depressions are formed when cold polar air meets warm tropical air and then a kink develops in the boundary which eventually becomes a circular movement of air. As they move north east they usually end up over Scandinavia and eventually die out. The cold air catches up with the warm air and pushes the warm air out of the way. When this happens the depressions is said to have **occluded**. Depressions have two areas called **fronts**, a warm one and a cold one. In the diagram the winds can be seen blowing anti clockwise round the centre of the low pressure centred over Northern Scotland. The warm front is indicated by the rounded bumps while the cold front is indicated by the sharper points. In between the warm and cold fronts is an area of air called the warm sector. This is an area of warm muggy weather, overcast with drizzle or fog and poor visibility. The winds around a low pressure area tend to be drawn into the centre of the depression and do not flow parallel to the isobars except in the warm sector. There is a definite weather sequence associated with the passage of a depression and the diagram shows what happens. Cirrus clouds will often indicate the approach of a depression, and as it approaches the cloud level becomes lower and eventually covers the whole sky.

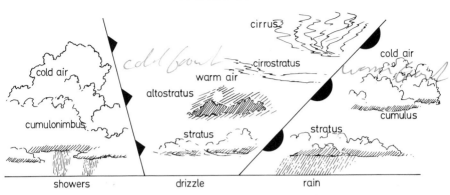

showers   drizzle   rain

Weather Forecasts

All information which is needed to make up a weather forecast for British waters is assimilated at the Meteorological Office in Bracknell, Berkshire. It is from there that the basic weather forecasts are given and distributed to the press, television and radio. Weather forecasting is not an exact science and errors can occur even with the sophisticated modern equipment. It is still not possible always to predict the exact course a depression will follow, or its speed or whether an established high pressure system will continue to keep a low pressure system at bay.

Shipping Forecasts for the sea areas around the British Isles are broadcast on BBC Radio 4 on 200Hz (1500m) long wave and on local MF frequencies at 0033 0555 1355 1750. These are clock times in use throughout the year.

Inshore Waters Forecasts are on Radio 4 on 200 Hz (1500m) at the end of the programmes for the day at about 0038 and also on Radio 3 1215 Hz at 0655 daily.

General Weather Forecasts are also transmitted by local radio stations many of which also give coastal waters forecasts. The times and frequencies of these forecasts can be found in nautical almanacs. These also give details of forecasts broadcast by adjacent European countries.

Telephone forecasts can be obtained from the coastguard stations,

regional weather centres or recorded information services, the numbers for all of which will be found in local directories.

Weather Instruments

A yachtsman should understand the common meteorological instruments, though it is not necessary to possess them all.

Barometer A barometer measures atmospheric pressure. It can give a good indication of impending weather and is the one instrument any well found yacht should have. A rapidly falling barometer with a backing wind or a rapidly rising barometer with a veering wind will indicate a gale. A falling barometer usually means worsening weather with stronger winds and rain, whereas a steadily rising barometer will indicate better weather is on the way. If the barometer remains steady with only slight fluctuations a settled period will ensure. A note needs to be kept of the readings to be sure you are interpreting them correctly.

Barograph This also measures pressure, but also records it as an ink trace on graph paper round a revolving drum. This gives you an immediate picture of the way the pressure is rising or falling and how quickly.

Anemometer An instrument which measures wind speed. It is usually mounted at the masthead and consists of cups which rotate when the wind blows and records on a dial in the cockpit the speed of the wind in knots.

Hygrometer This instrument consists of a wet and dry thermometer housed in a small ventilated box to measure the water vapour content in the air.

Listening To Shipping Forecasts

Shipping forecasts are essential to anyone making an offshore passage. General weather forecasts covering land areas do not give sufficient relevant information. Never rely on just listening to the weather forecast and remembering it. It should be noted and for preference plotted as described later. All shipping forecasts are given in a standard sequence and as they are also given at very high speed it is helpful to know the sequence which is as follows

Gale warnings, if any, stating in which sea areas.

General synopsis – the position of highs and lows and their direction of travel.

Forecast for individual sea areas giving wind direction and force, conditions and visibility.

Reports from coastal stations.

Gale warnings. These do not necessarily wait for the shipping forecasts but are broadcast at convenient breaks in programmes. They are however always repeated at the beginning of each shipping forecast. Gale warnings are issued when winds of force 8 or above are expected. They have their own terminology. A gale is said to be either

imminent (expected within 6 hours)

soon (between 6 & 12 hours) or

later (more than 12 hours)

Gale warnings are also broadcast by coastal radio stations and can be picked up on the VHF working frequency. Though visual signals in the shape of north and south cones are no longer displayed by coastguard stations as they were until a few years ago this system, or a local variant, is still operated by some yacht clubs, harbour masters and marinas.

Taking Down The Forecast. It is not sufficient to take down the forecast only for the sea area in which you are. You must note it all so that you are aware of the general situation. There is no time to take a longhand note and some form of shorthand or abbreviation is essential. Even so it takes practice to keep pace. The best way is to put the information straight down on an outline map of the sea areas. Pads of these can be purchased from chandlers.

Symbols. There are some recognised symbols for use in noting shipping forecasts. The most useful is the arrow which indicates wind direction. On each arrow are placed 'feathers' to represent the strength of the wind forecast in the Beaufort scale. These are drawn in half units – in other words a half stroke for force 1, a long stroke for force 2, one and a half strokes for force 3 and so on.

Reports from coastal stations. It is as important to take these down as it is the forecast. There are more than a dozen coastal stations round the British Isles. Actual (not forecast) conditions at each a few hours before the broadcast are given and this information can be used to construct your own present synoptic situation and forecast. It is not suggested that yacht skippers would be better at it than professional meteorologists, only that the additional picture of the weather situation this provides can be valuable. Each coastal station reports wind direction and strength, general conditions, visibility, the barometer reading and whether it is rising or falling. From the barometer readings it may be possible to draw in approximate isobars to reveal the weather system. Shifts in wind direction will show where the fronts are. Plotting these at home in comfort is good practice.

Interpreting Weather Maps

Several newspapers print daily synoptic weather charts. It is worth saving these for several days and pasting them together to study how the systems develop and the associated weather they bring. Some general points to remember are:
    The sequence of weather following fronts described earlier in this section.

Winds follow approximately the direction of the isobars, though in a low they will be pointing in a little more towards the centre.
The closer the isobars the stronger the wind.
Secondary lows developing on the edge of existing low pressure systems often give rise to winds of exceptional intensity with little warning

Land And Sea Breezes

In proximity to coastlines local conditions often occur which are not in accord with the wider weather forecast. Winds are caused by the heating of the land surface by day and the cooling of the land surface at night respectively. Sea temperature is affected little by the sun and probably changes by only a degree or so, but the land heats up considerably in comparison during the day. As it does so the warm air over the land rises pulling in colder air from the sea to take its place. The winds created can become quite strong during the afternoons and can blow up to force 5. They die down again as evening approaches. During the afternoon the winds will veer due to the rotation of the earth. At night the reverse takes place. The land cools rapidly under clear skies and so as the air is cooled by the cold land it becomes heavier and denser and so sinks and tends to flow down valley sides and out to sea. This land breeze is weaker than the sea breeze only reaching about force 2. It is most noticeable at sunrise in sea estuaries and so if an early start to the day is required it may be possible to take advantage of the land breeze to help you out to sea.

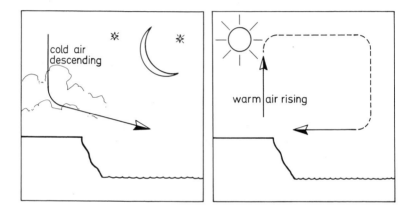

Forecasting Fog

Though difficult to predict it is helpful to know the conditions in which fog may occur.

Radiation fog (or land fog) This type of fog only forms over land, but can drift out to sea for a few miles particularly in estuaries. It seldom extends more than five miles offshore. The fog is caused by the land cooling on a clear cloudless night with little wind. The air will have a high relative humidity and a land surface which is cold and wet. The fog usually occurs at sunrise, and as the sun rises and creates warmth so the fog will disperse. In winter this type of fog can remain for a few days if the sun is not strong enough to disperse it.

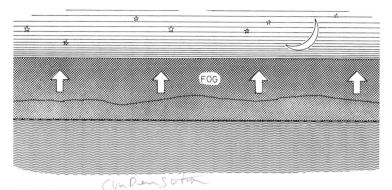

Condensation

Advection Fog (or Sea fog) caused by warm air moving over a cold sea. Before it can form the sea temperature must be below the dew point of the air. A frequent example is warm air moving from the European continent over the cold North Sea where it creates fog. Sea fog is also caused when air from over a warm sea moves over colder waters. It frequently develops where the warm waters of the Gulf Stream meet the cold Labrador current near Newfoundland. In spring and early summer warm moist air moving up from the Azores moves into the colder waters of the English Channel thus causing extensive fog in the Channel.

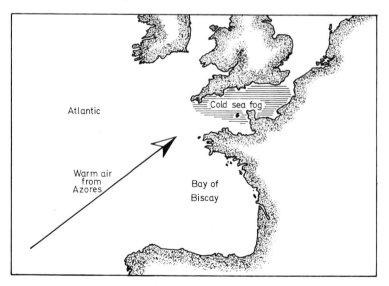

Frontal Fog Occurs at or near a front where warm and cold air is mixing. If the air is saturated or nearly saturated fog will form.

Questions

1 What are the times of the shipping forecast on Radio 4?
2 What does a barometer measure?
3 Name (a) two high clouds (b) two low clouds
4 What are (a) a front (b) a col (c) an occlusion?
5 What is (a) a backing wind (b) a veering wind?
6 When are gale warnings issued?
7 What are the following on the Beaufort scale. Light breeze 4 – 6 knots; fresh breeze 17 – 21 knots; gale 34 – 40 knots?
8 Describe the weather sequence associated with a depression
9 Name some conditions that cause fog
10 What weather is associated with a high pressure area?

15
ANCHORING

Types of Anchor

The ground tackle of a yacht needs to include two sorts of anchor:
The bower anchor. This is the main anchor of the vessel, normally permanently stowed on the foredeck and made fast to its cable ready for use. Large vessels may have two bowers, port and starboard, referred to in former times as the best and second bowers. In normal circumstances you will anchor with the bower alone.
The kedge anchor. A second and usually smaller anchor. Depending on space and facilities available it can be stowed away and not bent on until needed. It has a number of uses which include:

as a second anchor to supplement the bower in heavy weather
as a second anchor to prevent excessive swinging
as a stern mooring when laying head to a quay
to lay out with the dinghy to haul off a yacht aground
to lay out to warp off an engineless yacht.

As the kedge must often be taken out by dinghy the reason for its lightness will be seen. The type of anchor chosen will depend on the owner's personal preferences, the stowage room available and perhaps the nature of the bottom in the accustomed cruising grounds. Here is a brief recap of the main types.
Fisherman's. Sometimes called Admiralty pattern. The traditional type of anchor not now much in use in yachts. Good on a rocky bottom but not so efficient as others in sand and mud. Stows flat with stock unshipped but you need a much heavier one for the same holding power than other types.

CQR. Sometimes called a plough anchor from its shape. Oldest of the modern stockless anchors. Good digging action and holds well in sand and mud.

Danforth. Has twin flukes which dig in. Folds flat and very easy to stow. Same holding characteristics as CQR but will need a little more weight for the same holding power.

Meon. Similar to a Danforth, but with three flukes.

Bruce. A relatively new patent anchor shaped like a big claw. Better holding power weight for weight than other types. Holds well on most bottoms including rock. Might be awkward to stow on some yachts.

Chains and Warps

Chain is preferable to rope as an anchor cable. It is not always practicable on smaller craft because of weight and stowage problems, but if rope is used the efficiency of the anchor will be greatly improved if it can be combined with a few metres of chain at the anchor end.

Whether chain, rope or a combination the anchor cable is as important for holding power as the anchor itself. Anchors dig themselves into the ground as weight comes on them, but there needs to be sufficient cable paid out to lay along the bottom to exert a horizontal pull on the anchor. A vertical pull will break it out of the ground where it has no holding power. A good catenary or curve in the cable also acts as a shock absorber. Chain more easily assumes the desired shape because of its weight. Consequently it is usual to anchor with chain paid out to three times the depth of water, but with a rope warp five times the depth should be used.

Selection of Anchorage

Skippers should always have studied possible anchorages in advance. A number of factors will influence choice.

Weather. A good anchorage will need to provide shelter against any weather likely during the length of stay. An exposed lee shore should be avoided in strong winds and an eye needs to be kept on the forecasts against a shift of wind that might turn a snug anchorage into a lee shore.

Holding ground. Study the chart to find what sort of bottom there is. Sand and mud usually provide a secure hold, though the latter can sometimes be hard work to break the anchor out of. Shingle is not quite so good. Rock can result in difficulties with a foul anchor. Thick weed provides poor holding. The chart shows the type of bottom with abbreviations (m. for mud., sh. for shingle, etc). There will sometimes also be on charts a small anchor indicating a recommended anchorage and yachtsmen's pilot books also have advice about them.

Depth of Water. Before selecting an anchorage tidal calculations should be made to determine *check* SOUNDINGS

the depth of water when you anchor and therefore the amount of chain needed
how much chain you will need out at high water may have to leave someone
whether there is enough water to float you at low tide on the boat to
whether there will be enough water all round you as you swing with it help
change of wind and tide. chain not enough if
such a vertical pull.

Swinging room. Remember you will swing round your anchor with changes of wind and tide. There must be room for you to swing and others around you too. This can be difficult to judge in a popular anchorage. Better to have a longer row ashore than find yourself crashing against another craft in the middle of the night. The same also applies when anchoring near a fixed object such as a post or isolated rock.

Foul ground. These words sometimes appear on the chart and indicate a bottom with some debris or obstruction on which an anchor may become fast. Anchoring near underwater cables or pipelines should be avoided for the same reason. There is the same difficulty about dropping an anchor among permanent moorings which may have chain laid out along the bottom.

Other traffic. For peace and comfort as well as for your own safety and that of others always anchor well away from other craft on the move. Avoid busy fairways and narrow channels.

Reminders About Anchoring

The requisite amount of chain or warp should be on deck as you approach. Distinctive marks every fathom or two metres is the handiest way of knowing how much you have up. Always let go with a little way still on the vessel to help the anchor bite into the ground. If in doubt a few revs astern on the anchor will lay out the cable properly and help the hook dig in. Take care not to drop anchor over somebody else's anchor line. Before going ashore or relaxing below make sure the anchor has held. Find a transit ashore which will tell you if it is dragging, or take one or two bearings. If you go ashore keep an eye open for conditions changing. It doesn't take long for a smooth sea to change into a swell which makes it difficult to get back aboard quickly. It is often preferable to leave someone on board to let out more chain if necessary. International regulations (see next chapter) specify that vessels at anchor should show a black ball by day and a white light at night. Though more honoured in the breach some harbour authorities may insist on it. It is a prudent thing to do anyway if you are not in a harbour but anchored off a shore or in some isolated spot, especially at night.

Questions

1 How much chain would you pay out when anchoring?
2 What precautions would you take when anchoring?
3 Do you need to show an anchor light at night?

16

RULE OF THE ROAD

'The Rule of the Road' is a common expression for the International Regulations For Preventing Collisions At Sea. It is a subject on which Yachtmaster examiners expect candidates to have a sound and unhesitating knowledge, for when two vessels are on a collision course there is no time to refer to the rule book. Yachtmaster candidates are expected to be familiar with all 38 rules and with two of their four annexes. It is not essential to know them verbatim, but it helps to learn the most important passages in this way and to know just what they mean. You will find the rules printed in full in Reed's Nautical Almanac and also in the RYA booklet G2/83. They cannot be repeated in full here and the purpose of this chapter is to help you revise the salient points.

Part A. General

Rule 1. Application. *'these rules shall apply to all vessels upon the high seas and in all waters connected therewith navigable by seagoing vessels'*
This makes it plain that these are not just big ship rules. No vessels are outside the rules and they apply not just out at sea but up rivers and in harbours. Four following clauses make it clear that some harbour authorities or other proper bodies may have made special local rules to suit particular circumstances and it is the duty of the mariner to be aware of these. These will nearly always have been framed in close conformity with the international regulations.
Rule 2. Responsibility. *'nothing in these rules shall exonerate any vessel or the owner, master or crew thereof from the consequences of any neglect to comply with the rules, or of the neglect of any precaution which may be required by the ordinary practice of seamen or the special circumstances of the case'*

Although all masters (and that includes yacht skippers in this context) will have no excuse for not complying with the rules it is made clear that they cannot plead the rules as an excuse if they could have taken any action to avoid a collision. The next clause says that they shall have regard to all circumstances which may make a departure from the rules necessary to avoid immediate danger.

Rule 3. General Definitions. This rule defines just what is meant by some of the words used. *'The word "vessel" includes every description of water craft, including non-displacement craft and seaplanes, used or capable of being used as a means of transportation on water.'* (In other words the rules apply to sailboards as much as supertankers).

'Power-driven vessel means any vessel propelled by machinery.'
'Sailing vessel means any vessel under sail provided that propelling machinery, if fitted, is not being used' (if a yacht is running her auxiliary she is technically a powered vessel whether the sails are hoisted or not). A vessel engaged in fishing means any vessel fishing with nets, lines, trawls or other fishing apparatus which restrict manoeuvrability, but does not include a vessel fishing with trolling lines or other fishing apparatus which do not restrict manoeuvrability.

'Vessel not under command means a vessel which through some exceptional circumstance is unable to manoeuvre and is therefore unable to keep out of the way of another vessel.'
'Vessel restricted in her ability to manoeuvre' means a vessel which from the nature of her work is restricted in her ability to manoevure. Dredgers, cable-layers, tugs with a tow, would be good examples.
'The term "vessel constrained by her draught" means a power-driven vessel which because of her draught in relation to the available depth of water is severely restricted in her ability to deviate from the course she is following.' Typically this would be almost any large ship negotiating a harbour channel.
'The word "underway" means that a vessel is not at anchor, or made fast to the shore, or aground.' This makes it clear you don't have to be actually moving (i.e. making way through the water) to be underway.

Part B. Steering and Sailing Rules

Rule 4. Application. Says that the rules apply in all conditions of visibility.

Rule 5. Look Out. *'Every vessel shall at all times maintain a proper look out by sight and hearing . . .'* A crucial rule. It is easy on a yacht to forget that vision to leeward may be obscured by the sails and to rely solely on the helmsman. It also stresses importance of listening watch in bad visibility.

Rule 6. Safe Speed. All vessels to proceed at all times at a safe speed so they can take proper and effective action to avoid collision and be stopped within an appropriate distance. The rule lists all the factors to be taken into account in deciding a safe speed. They are visibility, traffic density, your own manoeuvrability, background light clutter, state of wind, sea and current, proximity of navigational hazards, and depth of water.

Rule 7. Risk of Collision. This rule underlines the skipper's responsibility to determine by all available means whether, whenever another vessel is in sight, a risk of collision exists. It stipulates that a risk shall be deemed to exist if the compass bearing of the other vessel does not appreciably change. It goes on to lay down that this is not fool proof. The risk may still exist when there is an appreciable bearing change, particularly approaching a very large vessel, or a tow, or at close range. Radar must also be used when available to check the collision risk.

Rule 8. Action To Avoid Collision. If you have to take action to avoid collision this rule says first that you must do it in good time and do it positively. You may do it by altering course or speed, or both, as the circumstances require, but the alterations must be large enough to be readily apparent to the other vessel. A succession of small alterations should be avoided. If there is plenty of sea room altering course alone should be sufficient providing it is done in good time and does not result in creating a fresh risk with another vessel. However a vessel should slacken speed, stop or reverse her engines if necessary. This rule also says that avoiding action must be such as to pass at a safe distance. It won't do just to clip under the stern of the other vessel.

Rule 9. Narrow Channels. A particularly important rule for yacht skippers as it governs conduct in traffic situations and in relation to commercial shipping. The first provision is that all craft must keep as far to the starboard side of the channel as is safe and possible. The fact that most yachts can conveniently do this is underlined by the next clause which states that no vessel of less than 20 metres length, nor any sailing vessel, shall impede the passage of vessels which can only navigate within the narrow channel or fairway. What constitutes a narrow channel is not defined, but what looks like a wide expanse of estuary to a yacht may be shallow water to a merchant ship. Anywhere with lateral buoyage would almost certainly constitute a narrow channel and a yacht may well be able to stay just outside the marks. The rules also lay down that you must never cross a channel in a way which will impede a deep draught vessel, never anchor in a channel or fairway unless forced by circumstances, or fish in one.

Rule 10. Traffic Separation Schemes. A complex rule which requires careful study of the full text. All shipping in a traffic separation zone must proceed in the appropriate lane in the general direction of the traffic flow, keep clear of the separation zone and normally only leave or join the lane at the termination points. One particular clause of interest to yachtsmen is that which stipulates that all craft under 20 metres and all sailing vessels may use the inshore traffic zones under all circumstances. Other vessels are enjoined not to use these if they can safely use the appropriate through traffic lane. The other important clause for yachtsmen is that which governs crossing separation schemes. This must be avoided if possible, but if necess-

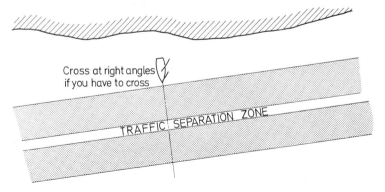

Cross at right angles
if you have to cross

TRAFFIC SEPARATION ZONE

ary must be done at right angles to the general traffic flow. Under sail in particular this raises the question of whether the rule means at right angles by bearing or by the actual track sailed. The intention is obviously that yachts should pass through the zone as expeditiously as possible and skippers encountering light airs or tacking against a headwind would resort to the motor to best comply with the spirit of the rules. It is also stipulated that no sailing vessels or any under 20 metres shall impede the safe passage of power driven vessels following traffic lanes – that means keeping well out of their way, never getting at close quarters or causing them to alter course.

Section 2. Conduct of Vessels In Sight of one another

Rule 11. Application. Simply makes it clear that the rules which follow apply when ships are in sight of one another.

Rule 12. Sailing Vessels. When any two sailing vessels are approaching each other so as to involve a risk of collision the one with the wind on the port side must get out of the way of the one with the wind on the starboard side. If they both have the wind on the same side the one to windward shall keep out of the way of the one to leeward. But if a yacht with the wind on the port side sees another to windward and cannot make out which side the other has the wind she shall keep out of the way. Finally to remove any doubts this rule defines 'windward' as being *'the side opposite to that on which the mainsail is carried, or in the case of a square rigged vessel, the side opposite to that on which the largest fore and aft sail is carried.'*

Rule 13. Overtaking. The first part of this rule puts responsibility on overtaking vessels in all circumstances. The overtaking rules override all others in the steering and sailing section. If you are overtaking another craft you automatically become the give-way vessel. It then goes on to define overtaking which is *'when coming up with another vessel from a direction more than 22.5 degrees abaft her beam'* where at night you would be able to see only her sternlight but neither of her sidelights. If in doubt about whether you are overtaking you are to assume you are and behave accordingly. Finally once you have become an overtaking vessel the responsibility remains yours until you are finally past and clear. Rule 13 applies as much to sailing yachts overtaking motor vessels as it does to power vessels overtaking.

Rule 14. Head On Situation. *'When two power driven vessels are meeting on a reciprocal or near reciprocal course'* both of them must alter course to starboard so that the two vessels pass port to port. This is, when you see another vessel coming towards you head on or nearly head on, so that by night you would see both sidelights. If you are in doubt about whether this is the case the rule says you are to presume it is and act accordingly.

Rule 15. Crossing Situation. When two power driven vessels are crossing so as to involve risk of collision the one which has the other vessel on her own starboard side must keep out of the way. It also says that she must not do so by crossing ahead of the other vessel unless this is absolutely unavoidable.

Rule 16. Action By Give Way Vessel. If you do not have the right of way and have a duty to keep clear you must do it by taking *'early and substantial action'*. Early means as soon as you are aware that the two vessels are on a collision course. Substantial means a big enough alteration of course so that it is quite clear to the other ship that you have altered.

Rule 17. Action By Stand On Vessel. If you are a stand on vessel (i.e. the one with the right of way) this rule gives you the positive duty to keep your present course and speed until all danger of collision has passed. However it says that you may manoeuvre as soon as it is apparent that the give way vessel has not taken appropriate action. And it then goes on to say that you must take action if you find yourself so close that action by the give way vessel alone will not be sufficient to avert collision.

Rule 18. Responsibilities between vessels. This rule governs the relationships between different types of vessels. It gives some right of way over others automatically except when required otherwise by rule 9 (narrow channels), rule 10 (traffic separation schemes) and rule 13 (overtaking).

Power driven vessels keep out of the way of any vessels not under command, restricted in their ability to manoeuvre, engaged in fishing and sailing vessels.

Sailing vessels keep out of the way of vessels not under command, restricted in their ability to manoevure or fishing.

Fishing vessels keep out of the way of vessels not under command or restricted in their ability to manoeuvre.

All vessels except those not under command or restricted in their ability to manoeuvre must avoid impeding the safe passage of a vessel constrained by its draught.

Though this rule may look long and complicated it is merely imposing a duty on those who can most easily take avoiding action to do so. It may not always be easy to recognise some of the vessels with priority mentioned, but they should be displaying the special shapes by day or lights by night specified in later rules.

Section 3. Conduct of Vessels In Restricted Visibility

Rule 19. Conduct of Vessels in Restricted Visibility. The first three clauses are about general conduct, making it plain that the rule applies to vessels not in sight of one another when navigating in an area of restricted visibility. It lays on them a duty to proceed at a safe speed and have due regard for the prevailing conditions. The fourth clause tells masters who detect another vessel in these conditions by radar alone to determine if a close quarters situation exists and to take avoiding action in good time. The fifth clause says that the skippers of all vessels which hear the fog signal of another vessel forward of the beam must reduce speed to the minimum consistent with being able to maintain her course, or stop altogether and to navigate with extreme caution until all danger is passed.

Part C. Lights and Shapes

See colour plates in conjunction with following section.

Rule 20. Application. The rules which follow about lights and shapes must be complied with in all weathers. Regulation lights must be displayed from sunset to sunrise and also in restricted visibility.

Rule 21. Definitions. The words seem obvious but the definitions are very precise and need learning.

Masthead light. White light showing unbroken through an arc of 225 degrees from right ahead to 22.5 degrees abaft the beam on either side.

Sidelights. Green light on starboard side. Red light on port. Each of them fixed to show from right ahead to 22.5 degrees abaft the beam.

Important proviso for yachts is that any craft of less than 20 metres may combine the sidelights in one lantern carried on the fore and aft centreline.

Sternlight. White light. Must be as near as practicable to stern and show through 135 degrees from right aft to 67.5 degrees on either side.

Towing light. Yellow light conforming to same rules as sternlight.

All round light. One showing unbroken through 360 degrees.

Flashing light. Means a regular flash at frequency of 120 per minute or more.

Rule 22. Visibility of Lights. The rule lays down the minimum distance at which lights must be visible in clear conditions.

Vessels more than 50 metres length. Masthead light 6 miles, all other lights 3 miles.

Vessels 12 to 50 metres. Masthead light 5 miles, all other lights 2 miles. But for those under 20 metres the masthead light visibility is 3 miles.

Vessels less than 12 metres. Masthead light 2 miles, sidelights 1 mile, stern, towing or all round lights 2 miles.

Rule 23. Power driven vessels under way. Power craft must show at night a masthead light forward, a second masthead light abaft of and higher than the first (this one optional if less than 50 metres), sidelights and sternlight. Air cushion vehicles (hovercraft) must also have an all round flashing yellow light. Power vessels of less than 12 metres are permitted instead of the above to show an all round white light and sidelights. If less than 7 metres (providing speed does not exceed 7 knots) the all round white is sufficient on its own, but sidelights should be exhibited if practicable.

Rule 24. Towing and Pushing. Specifies a variety of lights and day shapes which towing vessels and those being towed shall display. Candidates will be expected to know them.

Rule 25. Sailing Vessels. A sailing vessel under way at night must display sidelights and sternlight. If less than 20 metres length these may be in one combined masthead lantern. Optionally a sailing vessel may also exhibit near the masthead two all round lights, red over green, but not if the combined lantern is being used. Sailing craft less than 7 metres need only display the prescribed lights if practicable but must have a torch or lantern with a white light to show in sufficient time to avoid collision. Craft under oars may use

118

the same lights as sailing vessels but are not obliged to. However they must have at hand an electric torch or lantern. Sailing craft using engine with sails hoisted must show a conical shape, apex down, hoisted forward where it can best be seen.

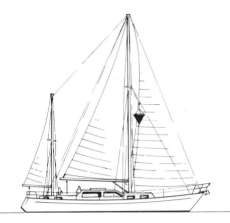

Sailing yacht using auxiliary showing a cone point downwards.

Rule 26. Fishing Vessels. A variety of lights and day shapes are prescribed for fishing vessels of different sorts to be used when fishing whether under way or not. There are more stipulated in Annex II for use when a large number of fishing vessels are working in close proximity. It is expected candidates will know them. Fishing vessels when not actually fishing show only the ordinary lights of a power vessel. The most important to remember are:
Trawler. All round green over white. By day two cones apex together. Under 20 metres a basket will do instead of the cones. If also under way masthead, stern and sidelights.
Other than trawling. Red over white. Otherwise as for trawler.
Rule 27. Vessels Not Under Command or Restricted In Their Ability to Manoeuvre.
Not under command. Two all round vertical red lights. Sidelights and sternlights if under way. By day two ball shapes vertically.
Restricted in ability to manoeuvre. Vertical lights red white red. When under way masthead, stern and sidelights in addition. By day a diamond shape between two balls.

119

There are a number of special provisions for particular vessels which come under the last category, including dredgers and those engaged in underwater operations.

Rule 28. Vessels Constrained By Their Draught. Three all round vertical red lights in addition to her normal steaming lights. By day a cylinder shape.

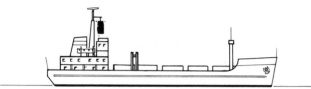

Vessel constrained by her draught exhibiting a cylinder

Rule 29. Pilot Vessels. White over red all round at the masthead. If underway side and sternlights in addition.

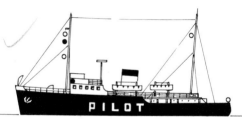

Pilot shows white over red in addition to normal steaming lights

Rule 30. Anchored Vessels and Vessels Aground. Vessels of more than 50 metres at anchor exhibit an all round white light in the fore part or a ball by day and a lower all round white light in the stern at night. Those less than 50 metres may at night show just an all round white light where it can best be seen. Ships over 100 metres must also use at night all available deck lights. Craft of less than 7 metres are exempt from showing anything at anchor providing they are not in or near a channel, fairway or anchorage where other vessels normally navigate. Vessels aground show two all round vertical red lights or three balls by day. Those less than 12 metres are exempted.

Rule 31. Seaplanes. They have to comply with the rules about lights as closely as they can.

Part D. Sound and Light Signals

Rule 32. Definitions.
Whistle. Any sound appliance capable of producing the prescribed blasts.
Short blast. About one second.
Prolonged blast. 4 to 6 seconds.
Rule 33. Equipment For Sound Signals. Vessels over 12 metres must be equipped with a whistle and a bell. Over 100 metres must have a gong as well. Under 12 metres it is specified only that there should be some efficient means of making a sound signal.
Rule 34. Manoeuvring and Warning Signals. Specified sound signals for power vessels under way as follows:
1 short blast – I am altering course to starboard.
2 short blasts – I am altering course to port.
3 short blasts – I am operating astern propulsion.

Other signals are laid down for use in a narrow channel or fairway:

2 long blasts 1 short – I intend to overtake on your starboard side
2 long blasts 2 short – I intend to overtake on your port side
1 long 1 short 1 long 1 short – I agree to being overtaken

If any vessel fails to understand another's intentions or is in doubt whether enough action is being taken to avoid collision it gives at least five rapid blasts. A vessel approaching an obscured bend gives a long blast in warning and can be answered by the same.

Rule 35. Signals in Restricted Visibility. These are for use in fog all the time, not just when a danger of collision is realised.

Power driven vessels sound 1 prolonged blast at least every 2 minutes when under way. *Sailing vessels* (in common with those not under command, restricted in ability to manoeuvre, constrained by draught, fishing, towing or pushing) sound 1 long 2 short every 2 minutes. *At anchor* all vessels ring a bell rapidly for 5 seconds at intervals of not more than 1 minute. Over 100 metres this must be rung forward, followed by a gong sounded rapidly aft. Additionally they may warn approaching vessels by 3 blasts (short-long-short). *Vessels aground* use the same signals as at anchor with the addition of 3 distinct separate strokes on the bell before and after the rapid ringing. All craft of *less than 12 metres* are exempted from the above but must make some other efficient sound signal at intervals of not more than 2 minutes.

Rule 36. Signals to attract attention. A short but important rule for sailing yachts. It says that any signal by light or sound made to attract attention must not be mistaken for any of the other signals in the rules or mistaken for any aid to navigation. It specifically forbids the use of strobe-type lights. Otherwise any means may be used, including directing the beam of a searchlight in the direction of the danger. But the rule says this must never be in such a way as to embarrass the other vessel – for instance not directly at the bridge if it would destroy night vision. For a yacht drawing attention to herself a short range light directed in the sails might be better, or a white flare.

Rule 37. Distress Signals. The rules lists 14 recognised methods of indicating distress and it prohibits the use of them, or anything which might be confused for them, for any other reason. They are all detailed in Annex IV as below.

Gun or explosive signal at one minute intervals
Red star rockets or shells
Continuous sounding of fog signal
SOS in morse
Mayday by radiotelephone
NC by international code flags
Any square flag with ball shape beneath
Flames from burning tar barrel or similar
Red parachute or hand held flare
Orange smoke signal
Slow and repeated raising and lowering of outstretched arms
Radiotelegraph alarm signal
Radio telephone alarm signal
Emergency position indicating beacons — could toss, then overboard.

Rule 38 and Annexes. Rule 38 deals with some technical points relating to ships about which candidates are unlikely to be questioned. Annexes I and III give detailed technical specifications regarding lights, shapes and sound signals, knowledge of which is not required. Annex II specifies the additional signals for fishing vessels and should be studied.

Study Annex IV

Questions

1 To which vessels do these rules apply
2 When may you depart from the rules?
3 Name some vessels restricted in their ability to manoeuvre
4 What does 'under way' mean according to the rules?
5 How can you check whether there is a danger of collision from an approaching ship?
6 If you have to give way what should you do?
7 Have you to do anything if you have right of way?
8 Two sailing yachts approach each other, both on the port tack. Which must keep out of the way?
9 A sailing yacht is overtaking a slow moving motor cruiser. Being under sail she has precedence. Right or wrong?
10 List the vessels a sailing yacht must give way to.
11 How far must the light of a vessels of 12–50 metres be visible?
12 What alternative lights are permitted for a sailing vessel of less than 20 metres.
13 If you saw at night a ship with a green light over a white light in addition to the port and starboard lights what would it be?
14 What would an approaching vessel with a flashing yellow light be?
15 A ship near you gives two short blasts. What does she mean?

17
SAFETY AT SEA

The skipper of a yacht is responsible for the safety of all on board. It is up to him or her to ensure that the vessel is properly equipped and safely conducted. Never must it be assumed that help will be forthcoming from rescue services if anything goes wrong.

Safety Equipment

There are no legal requirements for the equipment of privately used yachts but in order to establish some standards the RYA has drawn up a set of recommendations for craft of three categories. These are detailed in the RYA booklet C8/86 which should be studied. A brief summary for revision is given below, applying to yachts cruising offshore on passages over 50 miles.

Storm jib.
Storm trysail or means of reefing main to 60% full luff length
Sole purpose battery or starting handle for engine
2 anchors of appropriate size
Stem fairlead capable of closing over the warp or chain
Strong foredeck fitting (sampson post, mooring cleat or winch)
2 buckets with lanyards
Hand or electric bilge pumps
radar reflector
fixed navigation lights
foghorn
powerful torch or Aldis lamp
4 hand held red flares
2 buoyant orange smoke signals
4 red parachute rockets

4 hand held white flares
fire blanket
2 dry powder fire extinguishers 1.5kg min capacity
semi automatic fire system for engines over 25 hp
warm clothing, oilskins, seaboots for each person
lifejacket for each person
safety harness for each person
liferaft big enough for all on board
2 horseshoe lifebelts with drogue and automatic light
30 metres buoyant heaving line
boarding ladder
dan buoy AS A MARKER
radio receiver (for weather forecasts)
VHF radio telephone (desirable)
charts of intended and adjacent cruising areas
steering compass
hand bearing compass
navigational drawing instruments
barometer
lead line or echo sounder
radio direction finding set RDF
reliable watch or clock
first aid kit
towing warp
mooring warps and fenders
2 waterproof torches
dinghy (rigid or inflatable)
tool kits for engine, electrics, sail and general
spares for engines and electric equipment
bosun's bag (spare shackles, repair materials etc)
separate emergency water supply

Personal Safety

There should be lifejackets and safety harnesses for each member of the crew. They should all know where they are stowed and how to get into them. Due to differences in fitting everyone should adopt a lifejacket and harness and adjust it to their size at the beginning of a cruise, not rely on grabbing any old one as occasion arises.

Lifejackets. It is generally agreed that lifejackets which provide full personal buoyancy and keep the wearer afloat on his or her back, even if unconscious, are preferable for offshore cruising to buoyancy aids which are perfectly satisfactory for inshore day sailing. British Standard 3595 covers their manufacture, but there are reputable makes on the market which for various reasons have not been submitted for the BS kitemark. Lifejackets are cumbersome to wear and to work on deck in and most adults prefer not to wear them all the time. Skippers should consider requesting their use:

In heavy weather
At the onset of fog
Using the dinghy at night or in a choppy sea
During night watches
In the case of children, whenever on deck

Safety harnesses. More important in many respects than lifejackets, since they prevent you going overboard in the first place. It is essential they are used in conjunction with special clip-on points or to a lifeline running midships forward to aft and securely fixed. It is not a good idea to clip on to the guard rails as you can still fall overboard and be drowned or badly injured being dragged alongside. A hook-on point immediately inside the cockpit so that people coming up from below at night can be secure until they have got orientated is desirable. Safety harnesses should be worn:

For all work on deck, even in good conditions
By everybody not actually below at night, in heavy weather or fog
Most especially when there are only two people aboard (husband and wife sailing teams for instance)

Fire Risk

Fire at sea in a small vessel is a frightful prospect and prevention should be the prime consideration. See that the recommended extinguishers are carried, one placed near the engine compartment, one near the galley. A fire blanket should hang near the galley. Buckets with lanyards should be handy in a cockpit locker. Check the following precautions:

Brief crew on whereabouts of extinguishers and method of operation
Check gas and fuel installation regularly at joints and connections
Switch off both at source of supply when not actually in use
Ventilate bilges and engine compartment regularly. Fuel vapour and liquid gas are both heavier than air and sink into the bilges
Fit a gas detector low down
Keep firm control of smokers. Preferably confine smoking to the upper deck

If fire does break out the vessel should be stopped and all hatches closed to reduce air flow. Endeavour to tackle the flames with the extinguishers. For a galley fire the fire blanket may be more quickly effective. Buckets of water can be used in some cases, but never in the case of electrical fires or any involving petrol, diesel or cooking fat as water makes matters much worse. If it does not become quickly apparent that the fire can be brought under control the liferaft and/or dinghy should be prepared for launching and help summoned either by radio or visual communication with nearby vessels.

Distress Signals

In emergency there are many ways of summoning help. See under Rule 37 in previous chapter. All are for use in critical emergencies. They must only be used when life is in immediate danger. There are other procedures for requesting assistance when the difficulty has not developed to crisis point. Radio, morse and flag signals are dealt with in the section on communications. Flares, rockets and smoke signals may not be easy to light in emergency unless you have had experience of doing so. It is naturally difficult to practise with your own without the occasion being mistaken for an emergency, but there are short courses where they can be tried out and it is worth looking out for one. All these pyrotechnics should be kept in an accesible watertight container. They have a life of three years and must be renewed after that. If you are equipped with VHF you should maintain a listening watch on Channel 16 when at sea. Yacht skippers, just as much as professional seamen, have a duty to assist any vessel in distress if they can do so without endangering their own.

Coastguards

The coastguard service is responsible for initiating all search and rescue operations, both air and surface. They maintain a listening watch at 100 radio stations. They run a yacht safety scheme in which it is simple to participate. A card obtainable from any yacht club or harbourmaster is filled in giving plans of an intended voyage and identifying details of the yacht, together with the name of a contact ashore. If your shore contact does not receive a safe arrival message within a reasonable time of your ETA they can notify the coastguard who then has details of your intended course immediately to hand to guide any search.

Medical emergencies

A study of first aid is desirable for all skippers. An easy reference first aid book should be carried aboard. Some nautical almanacs have good sections on this subject. If it is not possible to reach port quickly and help is needed it can be summoned by a PAN PAN call on VHF (or if life is at risk a MAYDAY call), or the letter W ('I require medical assistance') in Morse or by international code flag.

Seasickness

An important safety subject as it can lead to serious crew weakness. Special pills like Stugeron can be effective, but need taking three times a day for 24 hours before sailing. Much can be done to reduce the likelihood including:

Avoiding alcohol, rich food and large meals before sailing
Not getting overtired
Keeping warm and dry
Being occupied on deck, particularly taking the helm
Starting a cruise with a short passage in moderate conditions

Man Overboard

The drill cannot be practised too often. Skippers should have worked out in advance exactly what they would do on any given point of sailing. One person must be told off immediately to do nothing but keep an eye on the person overboard and a finger pointing at them. They can be lost sight of within seconds. Lifebelts must be thrown swiftly and with accuracy to be any use. Having come alongside the person in the sea it is not easy to get them aboard. A line should be got round them as quickly as possible and a boarding ladder positioned.

Preparing For Heavy Weather

If heavy weather is forecast consideration must be given to seeking shelter if the skipper thinks that the experience of the crew is not up to coping with it. With a well found yacht and competent crew there is no reason why a passage should not be continued unless the forecast is for extreme conditions. Even if a decision is made to seek shelter it may not be reached in time and preparations must be made for withstanding the bad weather. If the nearest shelter is on a lee shore or a harbour of difficult or restricted entry it may be safer to stay at sea. Preparations needed are:

Reefing in good time before it begins to blow really hard
Extra lashings to secure the dinghy, anchors, boathooks and any other items on deck.
Secure all hatches and lockers
Fasten companion ways, skylights and portholes
Make up flasks of hot drinks before the galley becomes untenable
Prepare easy snacks, sandwiches, sweets, chocolate as cooking may be impossible
Put crew on deck into lifejackets, and/or harnesses as appropriate

It may be desirable to alter course to put you on an easier point of sailing or maintain sea room. Or heaving to may be more comfortable. In either event the chart should be checked to see what dangers there might be under your lee. If the shelter of harbour is chosen you will need to think what conditions might be like there when you reach it. Read it up in the pilot.

Question

1 What pyrotechnics should you carry on your vessel?
2 When would you expect yourself and your crew to wear a lifejacket?
3 How can the coastguard help you if you are in trouble?
4 Apart from taking pills how might you reduce risk of seasickness
5 Why is it desirable to ventilate the bilges regularly?

18

SIGNALS AND
COMMUNICATION

Yachtmaster candidates are expected to know the principles of signalling by Morse code and by flags, even though they may be equipped with radio. Radio communication requires a separate qualification but the basic procedures are outlined in this chapter.

Morse

The Morse code has served seafarers well the world over since its invention 150 years ago because its system of dots and dashes for letters and numbers is such a simple and versatile method of communication. Morse can be sent by any means of flashing light (normally an Aldis lamp, but a torch will do in emergency), by sound (especially before voice transmission over long distances was possible), or even by a waving flag (though this is now rarely practised). It is still a useful facility for seafarers, and an essential one for yacht skippers in respect of distress and assistance situations. As a minimum they should be able to send and recognise individual letters and their meaning in the international code of signals (see next section) and be able to recognise the identification letters transmitted by radio direction stations.

Learning Morse. There is no real short cut to learning Morse. Some people memorise groups of letters at a time. Others try to find related letters (e.g. E,I,S & H are all dots) or opposites to remember more easily. Lots of practise with a friend is the only way. Try to space your dots and dashes so that you can get an even rhythm going. Learn by sound as well as lamp so that you can use RDF sets easily.

132

Morse procedure. To attract the attention of someone you want to communicate with send a series of double A's – AA AA AA. The answering vessel will send a series of T's – TTTTTTT. You can then start your message. At the end of each word pause until the answering vessel sends a T to indicate they have understood. Or they may send RPT asking you to repeat the word. If you make a mistake send a series of E's – EEEEEEE – and then start the word again. At the end of your message send AR and the answering vessel will send R to show they have understood the whole.

International Code of Signals

The international code of signals is associated with a set of flags, each representing a letter or number. By hoisting them in groups a message can be sent. The much more important point however is that each letter of the alphabet when used alone also represents an important signal and the same letter can also have the same meaning when sent in Morse. It is therefore important to know the code even if you do not possess any flags. The beauty of the system is that the meaning is the same in any language. There is also a series of two letter signals conveying similar types of messages. With one exception (NC) knowledge of these is not expected but should you see a two letter hoist at sea it can be looked up in Reed's nautical almanac. The international code flags with their meanings and the equivalent Morse letters are shown in the colour plate section. All three should be memorised. The examiners particularly require familiarity with A D F J K L O Q T U V and the two letter hoist NC (I am in distress and require immediate assistance). Associated with the code letters are also the internationally recognised phonetics used for spelling out words by radio and these should also be learned. See the accompanying colour plates.

Flag Signalling

Few but the largest yachts carry a full set of international code flags, but skippers may wish to consider having a few for the more urgent or useful single letter signals. Everybody sailing to or returning from foreign ports must have Q.

To communicate by flag you must first hoist the special red and white code flag which is not a letter. The receiving ship hoists it in reply and then you can begin. The maximum number of flags that can be used in one hoist is four, so plain language messages are rarely sent. Usually the full code book is referred to as this enables a wide choice of messages to be made up on danger warnings, safety, medication and so forth. There are ten numeral flags and also three substitute flags which have to be used where a letter repeats. The receiving vessel uses the code flag to show that it has understood each group and the sender hoists it to signify end of message. The above procedures do not have to be followed to use one or two letter codes.

Flag Etiquette

Flags other than signal flags are in fact another means of communication insofar as they indicate to others nationality, membership of particular clubs in the case of yachts, or ownership in the case of commercial vessels. Regard for correct flag procedures is a hallmark of a responsible skipper.

Ensigns. These are flags of nationality. Some nations have variants of their national flag for use at sea. In the case of the United Kingdom these are the red, white and blue ensigns which were squadronal colours of the Royal Navy until the middle of the 19th century when they were re-allocated. The *white ensign* is used exclusively by the Royal Navy and members of the Royal Yacht Squadron. The *blue ensign* is granted by Admiralty warrant to some yacht clubs, used by some official organisations like HM Customs and by merchant vessels commanded by Royal Naval Reserve officers. In the case of yachts these ensigns must only be used when the warrant holder is actually on board. Some blue ensigns are 'defaced' with a device or insignia in the fly. The *red ensign* is that used by British merchant shipping and all privately owned vessels. It is therefore the ensign for all yachtsmen who do not hold a warrant for a special ensign.

In harbour ensigns should be hoisted at 0800 in summer, 0900 in winter and struck at sunset. They are then worn on an ensign staff at the stern. At sea some people take them in to save wear. In this case they must be displayed whenever entering or leaving harbour and in the presence of other shipping. The proper place for an ensign at sea was (and still is for vessels suitably rigged) at the peak of the gaff. Consequently some owners of Bermudian rigged yachts consider the ensign at sea should be worn two thirds of the way up the leach, but it is more convenient often to have it at the staff. Ensigns should not be used ashore, except by HM shore establishments – the union flag is the only proper one to use.

A salute with the ensign is sometimes expected or given as a mark of respect. In this case it is lowered to halfmast as you sail past and kept in that position until the saluted vessel dips in reply. You keep yours dipped until the other has re-hoisted. When yachts at sea were far less numerous than they now are it was de rigeur to salute all HM ships, royal yachts, foreign warships and flag officers of yacht clubs. In our relatively more busy cruising grounds skippers must use their common sense about what is appropriate. Far from land an exchange of courtesies between any two vessels passing close is always pleasant.

Burgee. Small flag, usually triangular depicting membership of a yacht club or similar organisation. It is equivalent to the commissioning pennant of a warship and should stay in place all the time at the mainmast truck. When the owner is a member of more than one club other burgees can be flown on the yardarm halliard, but the burgee of the club whose home waters he happens to be in will naturally take priority.

House flags. Used by shipping companies to signify ownership and flown from a yardarm. Some yacht owners like to indulge in personal house flags.

Courtesy flag. It has long been the custom of ships and yachts entering foreign ports to fly at the starboard yardarm the ensign of the country being visited. Not to do so may be taken as a sign of disrespect. If a national day or other important occasion is being celebrated during the visit it is customary to fly the host country's flag at the main.

Radio Telephony

Because VHF sets are becoming common on yachts it is essential that all users adhere to correct procedures so that there is not anarchy on the air waves. Owners must have a certificate before

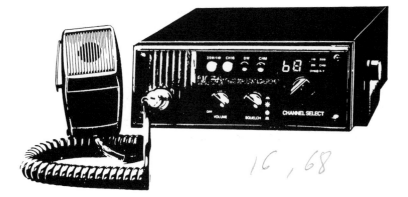

they may install a VHF radio-telephone and these involve an examination, but a knowledge of emergency drill is desirable for all yachtsmen. There are three categories.

MAYDAY calls, to be made strictly only when life is in serious and imminent danger. It can be made on behalf of another vessel in such danger. These calls are made in strict sequence on Channel 16.

(Call): MAYDAY MAYDAY MAYDAY
(Name): This is yacht Eileen May, Eileen May, Eileen May.
(Position): Two Three Zero degrees. Portland Bill two miles
(Nature of distress): Overwhelmed by heavy seas. Sinking.
(Assistance required): Need lifeboat or helicopter
(Other information): White yacht. Two adults, two children aboard
(Invitation to reply): Over

An interval should be left for reply. If none is forthcoming the message must be repeated at intervals. Yachts hearing a Mayday call are under an obligation to take action. This may mean acknowledging the call and proceeding to the assistance of the caller if practicable. If not, do not acknowledge but relay the message, having taken down the essential details of name and position, etc. The relay is made like a Mayday call but using the call MAYDAY RELAY, followed by your own name, then the name and position of the ship in distress.

PAN calls. Reserved for situations which are urgent but where life is not in imminent danger. You might for example have a medical

136

emergency and want to organise an ambulance at the nearest port you can make for. The call is PAN PAN PAN, followed by the ship's name and the nature of the emergency. This call will give you priority over all other callers on the air.

SECURITE calls. These are transmitted by the radio stations as a rule and used to issue important meteorological or navigational warnings. The words SECURITE SECURITE SECURITE are followed by a working frequency on which the message will be transmitted and it will be important to switch to it.

Questions

1 When should you fly a courtesy flag?
2 When should you fly an ensign?
3 Describe a Q flag and its meaning
4 When would you fly it?
5 What do the flags NC mean?

19

NAVIGATION IN RESTRICTED VISIBILITY

Fog at sea is a definite danger to be avoided if possible. To set sail when there is fog present or forecast is folly. Nevertheless it is capable of descending with alarming suddenness on the finest day and everyone gets caught in it at times. It is important to know what action to take. The official scale of visibility defines fog as being able to see less than 1,000 metres. Poor visibility is up to two miles, moderate up to five miles and good more than five miles. In fact, because of the low eye level, visibility from the average yacht is seldom more than three miles. Rain, drizzle, or heat haze all reduce it well below this, so most of us are sailing in poor visibility a lot of the time. The dangers of bad visibility are risk of collision, possibility of grounding and loss of visual navigation signs.

At The Onset of Fog

Position. Fix a position immediately. If in sight of visual navigation marks do it before they disappear in the murk. Back the fix up with radio bearings or running a line of soundings. Out of sight of land you will be better off if you have been keeping a good DR which you can convert to an EP.

Radar. Hoist the radar reflector if it is not already in place. But remember it is not an insurance policy against being run down. You are still difficult to spot from big ships. If you have your own radar set use it to spot other vessels, but not at the expense of neglecting visual look-out.

Look-out. In fog don't just leave it to the person at the helm. Put somebody else on the job as well, preferably up forward.

Crew Safety. Lifejackets and safety harnesses should be the order of the day. You would stand no chance of picking up a man overboard in fog.

Silence. In fog at sea it is golden. Your ears may give better warning than your eyes and if everybody is chattering you won't hear the approaching throb of an engine until it is too late. Or the breaking sea just before you hit a rock. If motoring switch off the engine every now and then to listen.

Sound signal. Sound your foghorn or make an alternative sound signal as required by the Collision Regulations, at least every two minutes. Listen out for those of others. If you hear one which seems forward of the beam stop until you are sure what it is doing. Don't rely on big ships being able to hear your signal, they probably won't.

Speed. Motor yachts may have to consider reducing to slow speed. Yachts under sail will rarely find this necessary.

Navigation In Fog

There are limitations to the reliability of navigational aids in fog. Sound signals from lighthouses may not be dependable for three reasons. It is difficult to judge just which direction the sound is coming from, the atmospheric conditions can muffle the sound, often quite close to the station, and sometimes they are not operating at all because they are triggered by light intensity and can be standing in bright sun while you are sailing in thick fog not half a mile away. Radio bearings can be suspect in similar conditions. All possible means of position plotting should therefore be used.

Skippers close to shore will face the decision whether it is safer to remain at sea or seek shelter. Running for harbour will be a chancy decision unless the entrance is wide and easy and even then there is increased risk from other traffic. If equipped with a radar receiver you may be able to feel your way in safely. Otherwise it is probably less risky to anchor close inshore away from busy channels. If the coast is approached at right angles taking careful soundings (providing there are no off-laying rocks) a hook can be dropped in shallow water (say five metres) where there will be no danger of being run down by big vessels. Avoid the shipping lanes at all costs. If you are crossing one when fog descends work your way out of it as cautiously as possible and alter course to avoid entering one until the fog lifts. When your decision is made maintain a steady course for as long as you can. Too many alterations of course with no chance of checking your position may result in faulty dead reckoning. Heaving to would not be wise as you want to keep some way on in case you have to take avoiding action.

Sound signals

Make sure you know the fog sound signals made by different vessels. These should not be confused with the sound signals made when manouvring in good visibility. The main ones are

1 prolonged blast every 2 minutes – power driven vessel under way
2 prolonged blasts every 2 minutes – power driven vessel stopped but under way (i.e. not at anchor or moored) *Io· not making way.*
1 long blast 2 short – variety of vessels under way including sailing vessels, fishing craft, vessels not under command or constrained by their draught, tugs and tows, etc.
Any efficient sound signal at 2 minute intervals – optional for any craft under 12 metres in place of the appropriate signal above.
Rapid bell ringing – ship at anchor.

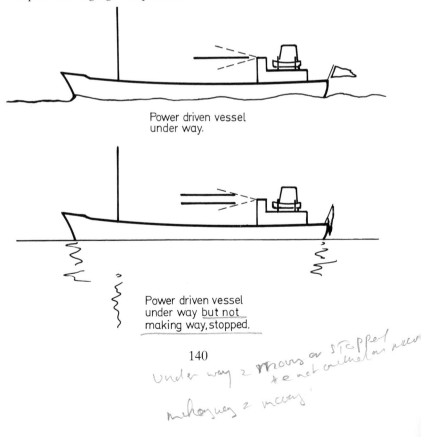

Power driven vessel under way.

Power driven vessel under way but not making way, stopped.

Under way 2 moves or stopped. not making way

making way 2 moving.

Questions

1 List some precautions when navigating in fog.
2 What is the fog signal for a sailing vessel under way?
3 If you hear a fog signal ahead of you what would you do?
4 What does the rapid ringing of a bell denote?
5 What signal do the rules permit vessels of less than 12 metres to make?

20

PASSAGE PLANNING AND MAKING

Planning a cruise and planning a passage are two distinct and separate tasks and should not be confused. A cruise (or voyage if it is on a more ambitious scale) consists of the routes to all the places you intend to visit. Of course you will want to read up about them to get some idea of navigational difficulties the itinerary may present, to order the charts you need and work out whether the distances are feasible in the time available to you. A passage is the journey from one port to another (whether that happens to be from Bridlington to Scarborough or from Falmouth to New York) and each one needs planning in detail.

Preparation Of Charts

These should be put in their folder in order of use for the passage. On top will be a small scale chart showing the whole passage and last a large scale harbour chart for the planned destination. They should all have been corrected up to the latest Notices to Mariners. If they have been used before all the old workings must be carefully rubbed off.

At any time in advance of the passage the skipper or navigator should make a note of all the principal navigation marks to be passed on the way and all hazards which his course will have to avoid. A notebook with this information can be kept handy on deck. It is easier to consult when checking the identity of an object than having to go below and look at the chart every time. The notes would include possible sources of radio bearings and useful transits.

Prior to sailing a chosen course should actually be laid on the chart, with a note made of the bearings for each leg. It may not be possible to adhere to this course, particularly when sailing, but you

142

will know that this is the course that has to be made good. The course line will enable you to measure the distances involved and so estimate your time of arrival (ETA) though this will naturally be subject to conditions of wind and tide which you do not at this stage know. When you have decided the time of departure it is a good idea to mark in on the course what you estimate will be the hourly DR positions to give you a ready check on whether progress is good enough to enable you to stick to your original plans.

Passage planning will also include making a note of possible contingency havens – what alternative anchorages are available to you in the event of severe weather or because you don't want to prolong a tediously slow passage in a calm, and can they be entered at all states of the tide? On the day you can also enter the times in the hourly boxes of the tidal stream atlas and work out how the tide is likely to affect your passage. Lastly draw in clearing lines on the chart for the ports you are leaving and entering and make a note of any leading marks.

Before Leaving

It is wise to have a check list to go through before you actually leave. It would include:

Last minute weather report. It may amend your plans.
Provisions adequate for longer passage than you intend.
Fuel and batteries topped up.
Adequate fresh water.
All charts and publications on board.
Engine starting without hesitation.
Crew fit and properly briefed.
Safety equipment checked.
Loose gear lashed on deck.
Coastguard notified of passage.
Customs cleared.
Navigation lights and other electrics working.

Customs Regulations

All yachts arriving in or departing from the United Kingdom are subject to customs regulations and it is the skipper's responsibility to see that they are obeyed. There can be heavy penalties for non-compliance. British yachts cruising foreign can be registered on the RYA Small Ships Register which satisfies the authorities in the case of private pleasure craft carrying less than 12 persons.

Before departure. Complete the customs form C1328 Notice of Intended Departure and take or send it to the nearest custom's office. It is only valid for 48 hours so if you delay beyond that they must be notified. If you abandon the plan altogether parts 2 & 3 of the form must be completed. Everybody on board must have a valid passport. In some countries proof of the yacht's registration and the skipper's certificate of competence will be demanded. If you are off on an extended cruise you may be entitled to take on bonded duty free stores, but this needs arranging well in advance.

Returning From Foreign. Fill in part 2 of form C1328. Hoist the Q flag as you enter territorial waters, illuminating it at night if possible. Within two hours of making fast notify customs of your arrival either in person or by telephone. This may be done by VHF telephone when in port, but not while still at sea. If there has been no visit from a customs officer after two hours of notification it is permissible to deliver or send the declaration form if there are no complications. This is known as a 'quick report'. The crew may then go ashore, but not until. A 'long report' is required if there are any goods on board on which duty is payable, any modifications or alterations have been made to the yacht abroad, there are any animals on board, anyone on board who does not have a British passport, if there has been any death or sickness or if you have been gone from the UK for more than a year. If you arrive between 2300 and 0600 it is permissible to delay reporting your arrival until 0800.

Passage routines

Even on the smallest family boat it is well to have some on passage routine for the sake of efficiency and safety. The first task will be to take a departure as soon as you are clear of harbour and out to sea.

C 1328 PART I

PLEASURE CRAFT BASED IN THE UNITED KINGDOM
PART I: FOR USE AS NOTICE OF INTENDED DEPARTURE TO A FOREIGN DESTINATION

1 Name of Vessel	2 Registration No.	Description (e.g. sloop, ketch, etc.)	Colour of Hull	Colour of Hull Band	6 Sail number

18

7 Length in metres	8 Tonnage	9 When built	10 Usual moorings or berth		11 Is vessel on hire, charter or loan	YES / NO

12 Name and Address of Owner

Has UK VAT been paid on
13 Vessel
14 All its equipment
YES / NO

Has UK VAT been deducted on
15 Vessel
16 Any equipment
YES / NO

17 If UK VAT has been deducted please state VAT Registration Number

19 Name and Address of Person Responsible if not owner

20 Place of departure	21 Date of departure	Time of departure

22 Destination

23 Expected date of return
If not known, please indicate. ✓

24 Expected Port of Return

25 Are animals or birds including domestic pets to be taken on the outward voyage?
If YES give details: —
YES / NO

I declare that the particulars given above are true to the best of my knowledge and belief.

Signature of person responsible (Departure) .... Date ....

HOW TO COMPLETE THIS NOTICE OF INTENDED DEPARTURE

1. Before your departure complete details on the face of Part I. Detach Part I and deliver or send it to the appropriate Customs and Excise office. (See Appendix 'C' of Notice 8 "Notice to Owners and Persons responsible for Pleasure Craft based in the United Kingdom".)

2. Retain Parts II and III on board.

3. If you do not reach a foreign destination, please write "VOYAGE ABANDONED" across the face of Part II and despatch both Parts II and III to the Customs and Excise office to which you sent Part I.

4. If duty-free ship's stores are to be taken on board the procedure in paragraph 2 of Notice 8 is to be followed.

WARNING: THERE ARE HEAVY PENALTIES FOR MAKING FALSE DECLARATIONS

FOR OFFICIAL USE ONLY

PERSONS ON BOARD

Name and Initials	Passport No.	Date of Birth	Nationality

3 Description of vessel

4 Colour of hull

5 Colour of hull band

32 No of P

33 No of N-P

34 Is it sailaway? YES / NO

To be finally exported by .... YES / NO

35 Visited

36 Collection of Departure identifier

37 Is No.38 overleaf completed YES / NO

Date form to NPCCU ....

Officer's Signature ....

Office of Departure date stamp

C 1328

F 4911(Jan 1985)

" / " as necessary

145

This fix will be the start of your navigation. Thereafter you may want to take a position or plot your EP every one or two hours according to conditions. You will also want to be aware of the time of the next shipping forecast – an alarm clock can be quite a handy piece of yacht equipment when the crew are all absorbed in their different tasks or their enjoyment of the sail. It is a good idea to allocate duties to everybody according to their experience and also to see that everbody has a chance of gaining more experience by a spell at steering, sail handling, navigating or whatever. On longer passages it is necessary to divide the crew into watches to ensure that nobody becomes over tired. Traditional watches are of four hours, split into half hour periods, but any pattern suitable to the people involved can be arranged. It helps however if a watch bill is written out so everybody can see what they have to do. For night passages two people should be the minimum in a watch, though if the complement is only two this is impossible and short watches are usually better in this case. Each watch should have an experienced member appointed as watch leader but the skipper should make plain the circumstances in which he wants to be roused. Watch leaders must fully brief their reliefs about the course being steered, lights in view, sightings expected, the present position, etc. and give them time to adjust to night vision before disappearing below.

Course Laying Strategy

The first essential of all courses is that they should be well clear of all dangers. Only close study of the charts can ensure this. On a normal coastwise passage a distance off of two miles should be regarded as a safe minimum, but you may have to be further out to avoid some of the tide races off headlands. Remember also that tidal set and leeway may put you much closer to rocks, wrecks, shoals, buoys, etc than you reckoned and allow for margins of error. Also important is the tidal set into bays which you should allow for when plotting headland to headland courses.

If you do not wish to pass closer than two miles to a headland a good way of finding an accurate course is to draw the arc of a circle at two miles radius round the objective and then draw your course line tangental to it. Your alter course position should be when the headland bears at right angles to the course line, unless there are

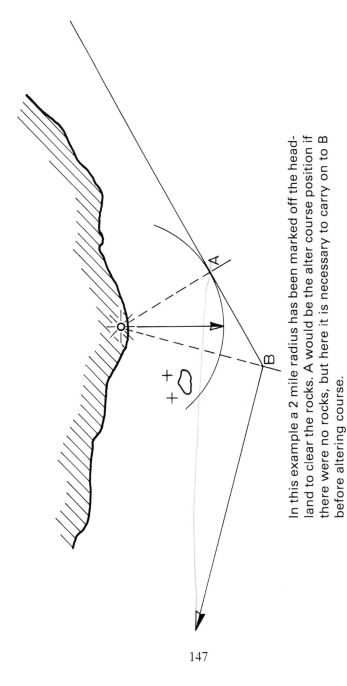

In this example a 2 mile radius has been marked off the head-land to clear the rocks. A would be the alter course position if there were no rocks, but here it is necessary to carry on to B before altering course.

other dangers to be avoided in which case you may need to maintain the original course longer. In the figure shown here the curve has been drawn at two mile radius and if there were no rocks the alter course position would be at A, but in this case the vessel will have to carry on until B before altering course.

Try to make alterations of course at places where you can easily establish your position rather than on the strength of DR. Double check courses laid off on the chart. It is very easy to make an error of 10 degrees or so. In an estuary or channel in poor visibility it is worthwhile to lay off courses from buoy to buoy – even in your home port this may be necessary to get you back to your moorings.

Course strategy will inevitably be affected by tide and the timing calls for some planning. The offshore flow of tidal stream may be more important than having the ebb to take you down river to the sea. It is no good, for instance, getting up early to catch the tide out of harbour only to punch a foul stream sailing along the coast. Maybe you could have left later and had a two knot stream helping you on your way. Plan the tides to give you as much help as possible. You may need to time things so that you arrive at your destination with a flood tide to get you in of course. Or you may be able to modify your course to gain a more favourable tide.

For sailing vessels the wind strength and direction will also influence course strategy, though this cannot reliably be anticipated. A desired course to windward can be made good by even tacks to either side of the course line, but it is often the case that one tack is more advantageous than another because of the lee-bowing influence of the tide and skippers may decide to make long and short boards.

Questions

1 What responsibility do you have towards the customs?
2 If you are planning to sail to France what documents would you need?
3 When you arrive back in the U.K. what should you do concerning customs?

ADDITIONAL EXERCISES

Use Admiralty practice chart No 5052 (Dover Strait)

1 A vessel is on passage from the Hamble to Dover and observes Beachy Head Lt bearing 333 (T) and Royal Sovereign Lt bearing 051 (T). Plot the vessel's position and give the latitude and longitude.

2 A vessel steeering north off the French Coast observes Le Touquet Lt bearing 130 (T) and C.d'Alprech Lt bearing 040 (T). Plot vessel's position.

3 A vessel steering 240 (T) observes the Royal Sovereign Lt bearing 270 (T) log reading 26. 1 hour later Royal Sovereign Lt bore 315, (T) log reading 30. Assume no current. Plot vessel's position.

4 HW Dover (Springs) 1200 hrs. A vessel steering due north (T) at 1600 observes Pte du Haut Banc Lt bearing 045 (T) log reading 20. At 1700 hrs the same light bore 090 (T) log reading 23.5. How far off the light is the vessel at 1700 hrs, using tidal diamond M?

5 In thick fog steering 060 (T) between Beachy Head and Dungeness. A radio D/F bearing of Dungeness gave 039 (T) and at the same time a radio D/F bearing of Royal Sovereign gave 272 (T). The sounding by echo sounder was 35 metres. Give the probable position of the vessel and the radio identification of the two lighthouses.

6 A vessel is making a passage from St Valery-sur-Somme to Boulogne. At 0845 Pte du Hourdel is abeam to port distance 2 cables and she sets course to pass close to red & white buoy in the Paie de Somme. Lay off true courses passing no closer than 2 miles to the coast to Boulogne. State also the compass courses. Find the total distance and estimate the ETA at speed 4 knots. Assume variation SW and no deviation.

7 At 1030 Pte du Haut Banc Lt. Ho bore 035 (C) log 8, and at 1130 Pte du Haut Banc Lt. Ho bore 095 (C) log 12. Is the vessel inside the course line?

8 Vessel continues on course and at 1330 Le Touquet Lt bore 116 (C) and the Gp Occ Lt bore 084 (C), log 20. What is vessel's position? What is new course to steer to make position 2 miles off C.d'Alprech Lt allowing for tide at H? Allow vessel's speed 4 knots.

9 At 1530 C.d'Alprech Lt. Ho. bore 095 (C) and a vertical sextant angle gave 0° 58′. How far off the lighthouse is the vessel?

10 What is course to steer from here to make Boulogne southern breakwater entrance? When you arrive an additional green light is showing from West entrance. What does it mean?

11 At 0800 a vessel is in position 5′ due south (T) of Royal Sovereign Lt. Find the true course to steer to a position 2 miles due south of Rye Bay buoy allowing for tidal stream at A. (HW Dover 1200 – springs) Vessel's speed 5 knots. Wind is S'ly force 5, allow 10° for leeway.

12 A vessel is steering down Channel on a true course of 245. At 1800 she leaves Vergoyer SW Buoy ½ mile to starboard. Vessel's speed estimated at 4 knots. What compass course should the vessel steer until midnight, allowing a compass error of 7W and tidal effect at L. (HW Dover 1200 springs) Wind is NW force 4, allow 5° for leeway.

13 At 1000 hrs a vessel is 1 mile due west (T) of C.d'Alprech Lt. Find the compass course to steer to the Vergoyer E. buoy allowing for tidal stream at H (HW Dover 0800 – Springs). 10° leeway is allowed for a force 6 SE'ly wind. Compass error 6W, vessel's speed 6 knots.

ANSWERS

Chapter 1 – Dead Reckoning and Estimate Position

1 Portland Bill 50 31N 2 27W, St Catherine's 50 35N 1 18E, Start
   Point 50 13N 3 38W
2 Because the meridians of longitude converge towards the poles,
   thus giving different measurements for each minute of longitude
3 6080 feet, 1,853 metres or 1.15 statute miles
4 Course and speed   *Tidal set / current*
5 Course and speed, plus any current and leeway

Chapter 2 – Position Lines

1 Compass bearings, radio bearings, soundings, transits, sextant
   sun sight
2 By taking a meridian altitude
3 That the vessel is at some point on the chart along that line
4 Two or more position lines crossing
5 It is free of compass errors

Chapter 3 – The Magnetic Compass

1 The amount a compass needle is deflected from true north due to
   the earth's magnetic field
2 Electric wiring, ferrous metal objects, vessel lying in one direction for a long period
3 Recording the amount of deviation of a ship's compass by comparing compass bearings on different headings wih true bearings
   on the chart

4 12 W
5 7 W
6 185
7 62

Chapter 4 – Position Fixing

1 Three bearings not meeting exactly but forming a small triangle
2 By measuring a vertical sextant angle which can be used with the known height of the light to find a distance off in table in the nautical almanac
3 Running fix, four point bearing, doubling the angle on the bow
4 Difficulty of positive identification, possibility of their being off station
5 Bearing on the beam of a lighthouse which is just appearing over or dipping below the horizon

Chapter 5 – Tides

1 1201 BST 6.3 metres
2 0849 BST 0.9 metres, 2109 BST 0.8 metres
3 HW 0106 BST 7.2 metres, 1330 BST 7.4 metres
   LW 0819 BST 0.9 metres, 2039 BST 0.8 metres
4 HW 0134 BST 5.6 metres, 1358 BST 5.6 metres
   LW 0906 BST 0.8 metres, 2122 BST 0.7 metres
5 1.3 metres
6 2 metres
7 1.2 metres
8 No

Chapter 6 – Tidal Stream

1 Nautical almanacs, charts, tidal stream atlases
2 A tide tip caused by obstruction of sea bed
3 Around headlands

Chapter 7 – Buoyage

1 Buoys which mark a channel
2 Black and yellow with topmark showing two cones apex up
3 To the north
4 Yes, with caution
5 To starboard. It is a port hand buoy on entry

Chapter 8 – Lights

1 Light characteristic, colour, height, range, sound signals
2 Constant light interrupted by brief periods of darkness
3 Nautical almanacs, Admiralty List of Lights
4 A light making a group of six flashes every 30 seconds
5 The maximum range a light can be seen in perfect conditions allowing for its height and the curvature of the earth

Chapter 9 – Pilotage

1 Lines drawn on the chart to clear all dangers
2 To help you enter harbour safely
3 Look out for shoal banks, other traffic, buoys. Have anchor and mooring lines ready

Chapter 10 – Echo Sounders

1 Sends electronic signal to sea bed
2 Approaching land or shoal waters, to help fix a position and as a precaution in fog
3 A useful standby if electronic sounders fail

Chapter 11 – Radio Aids to Navigation

1 By obtaining a null from a radio signal
2 A magenta circle
3 A position of navigational beacons and buoys

4 Immediate fixed position, course to steer and ETA
5 They are subject to errors of night effect, especially at long range, coastal refraction, half convergency and quadrantal error

Chapter 12 – Speed and Distance

1 Towed and impeller
2 Doppler
3 May be fouled with weed or line may entangle propellers

Chapter 13 – Deck Log

1 Yes, if it is signed and witnessed
2 Course, log reading, wind strength and direction, barometer, times of departure and landfall, times of passing navigational marks

Chapter 14 – Meteorology

1 0025, 0555, 1355, 1750
2 Air pressure
3 (a) cirrus, stratus; (b) cumulus, cirro cumulus
4 (a) a boundary of a cold or warm air mass; (b) an area between two highs and two lows; (c) when a cold front catches up with a warm front
5 (a) change of wind in anti-clockwise direction; (b) change of wind in clockwise direction
6 When winds of force 8 or more are forecast
7 Force 2; force 5; force 8
8 Cirrus clouds, stratus clouds, then rain and drizzle followed by clear skies and cumulonimbus clouds with wind increasing and backing, then veering and becoming steady
9 Land cooling at night, warm air over cold sea, mixing of warm and cold air
10 Clear skies, little wind, little precipitation

Chapter 15 – Anchoring

1 Three times depth of water. A rope anchor warp needs five times
2 Check sufficient depth of water at subsequent states of tide, sufficient swinging room, not over moorings over somebody else's anchor cable. Take bearings to check anchor is holding
3 White light hoisted forward in open water. In harbour if requested

Chapter 16 – Rule of the Road

1 To all vessels navigating on the seas and waters connected to the seas anywhere in the world
2 To avoid immediate danger if necessary
3 Cable layer, tug, dredger, aircraft carrier, minesweeper
4 Not an anchor or made fast to the shore or aground. It may be underway and not necessarily moving through the water
5 By taking bearings. Danger exists if they do not alter rapidly and substantially
6 Take action early and positively. Alterations of course should be substantial and take you well clear
7 Maintain course and speed, but be prepared to act if action of give way vessel alone will not avoid collision
8 The one to windward
9 Wrong. Overtaking vessels have obligation to keep clear in all circumstances
10 Vessels not under command, restricted in their ability to manoeuvre or fishing
11 Masthead 5 miles (3 miles if under 20 metres), side and sternlights 2 miles
12 Side and sternlights may be combined in one masthead lantern
13 A trawler
14 A hovercraft
15 She is turning to port

Chapter 17 – Safety At Sea

1 4 red flares, 2 smoke signals, 4 red rockets, 4 white flares
2 Rough weather, at night or in fog

3 Use of small boat safety scheme
4 Prior to sailing avoid alcohol, rich food, over-tiredness. At sea keep warm, dry and occupied
5 Both cooking gas and fuel are heavier than air and sink into bilges where they are potentially explosive

Chapter 18 – Signals and Communication

1 On entering the waters of another country
2 At sea and when in harbour from 0800 (summer) 0900 (winter) until sunset
3 Yellow flag meaning 'My ship is healthy and I request free pratique'
4 On arriving from a foreign port
5 'I am in distress and require immediate assistance'

Chapter 19 – Navigation In Restricted Visibility

1 Avoid traffic lanes, hoist radar reflector, reduce speed, sound fog signal, crew into lifejackets
2 1 long and 2 short blasts every 2 minutes
3 A ship at anchor
4 Any efficient sound signal every 2 minutes

Chapter 20 – Passage Making and Planning

1 Report arrival and departure
2 Proof of ownership and identity, passport
3 Report by phone or radio that you have arrived

Additional Exercises

1 50°39.4′N 0° 18′.5E.
2 50°36.2′N 1° 26.3′E
3 50°41.4′N 0° 29.2′E
4 3.4 miles
5 50°43.8′N 0° 43.3′E DU RY (possible D/F error ± 5 degrees)
6 Pt Hourdel to Buoy 281 (T) 286 (C) 3.6 miles.
buoy to C.d'Alprech 000 (T) 005 (C) (allowing for tide) 28 miles.
C.d'Alprech to Boulogne. Anything from 040 to 070 would do.
3.7 miles. ETA at Boulogne 1645.
7 Yes, she is about 0.4 miles inside course line.
8 50° 32.1′N 1° 31.9′E New course to steer 351 (T) 356 (C).
9 2 miles
10 043 (T) 048 (C) All vessels stop except one given permission to
enter.
11 046 (T) with leeway
12 265 (C)
13 219 (C)

INDEX

OTHER BOOKS FOR YACHTSMEN FROM DAVID & CHARLES

Topsail and Battleaxe
by Tom Cunliffe
A voyage in the wake of the Vikings
1988 Book of the Sea Award

Astro Navigation by Calculator
by Henry Levison

Exercises in Pilotage
by John Anderson

The Sailing Cruiser Manual
by John Mellor

Ocean Cruising Countdown
by Geoff Pack

One Watch At A Time
by Kim Nouak

The Shell Book of Seamanship
by John Russell

Shipshape: The Art of Sailboat Maintenance
by Ferenc Maté

Start With A Hull: Fitting Out A GRP Hull From Start To Finish
by Loris Goring

The Story of Yachting
by Ranulf Ragner & Tim Thompson